Italy

Italy

BY JEAN F. BLASHFIELD

Enchantment of the World™
Second Series

CHILDREN'S PRESS®

An Imprint of Scholastic Inc.

New York   Toronto   London   Auckland   Sydney
Mexico City   New Delhi   Hong Kong
Danbury, Connecticut

Frontispiece: **Florence skyline**

Consultant: David I. Kertzer, Professor of Anthropology and Italian Studies, Brown University, Providence, Rhode Island

Please note: All statistics are as up-to-date as possible at the time of publication.

Book production by The Design Lab

Library of Congress Cataloging-in-Publication Data
Blashfield, Jean F.
  Italy / by Jean F. Blashfield.
      pages cm.—(Enchantment of the world. Second series)
  Includes bibliographical references and index.
  ISBN 978-0-531-23677-2 (lib. bdg.)
 1. Italy—Juvenile literature. I. Title.
  DG417.B583 2013
  945—dc23   2013000087

Gondolier in Venice

Contents

CHAPTER 1   Introducing Italy................................... **8**

CHAPTER 2   Exploring the Boot............................. **14**

CHAPTER 3   Natural Italy **28**

CHAPTER 4   The Story of Italy............................... **38**

CHAPTER 5   Governing the Republic........................ **60**

CHAPTER 6 Making a Living **70**

CHAPTER 7 People and Language **84**

CHAPTER 8 A Catholic Nation **92**

CHAPTER 9 Cultural Life **102**

CHAPTER 10 A Stroll Through Italian Life **116**

Timeline **128**

Fast Facts **130**

To Find Out More **134**

Index **136**

Left to right: **Carnival, Naples, Colosseum, La Befana race, olive tree**

CHAPTER 1

Introducing Italy

A CAR HORN BLASTS, AND ROBERTO OPENS HIS EYES. He hops out of bed, goes to the window, and looks out at the bright Rome morning. Rome, the capital of Italy and his hometown, is always bustling. Roberto dresses, brushes his teeth, and heads to the kitchen for a quick breakfast of milk and chocolate biscotti, hard, crunchy cookies. He then races down the stairs and outside into a narrow alleyway. Two motorized scooters called Vespas zip by, while a small car maneuvers carefully to get past parked cars. Roberto soon meets his friend Gianni, and they walk to school, chatting excitedly about the big soccer game this weekend. Roma, their home team, is playing Milan.

School starts at 8:30 a.m. The first class is history, Roberto's favorite. Today, they are learning about the Etruscans, people who lived in the region more than 2,500 years ago. Snack time at school is 11:00 a.m. Roberto unwraps a piece of simple white pizza. It has both mozzarella and ricotta cheese, but no tomato sauce. After snack, they study math and English.

Opposite: **Traffic races by the Colosseum, an ancient ruin in Rome.**

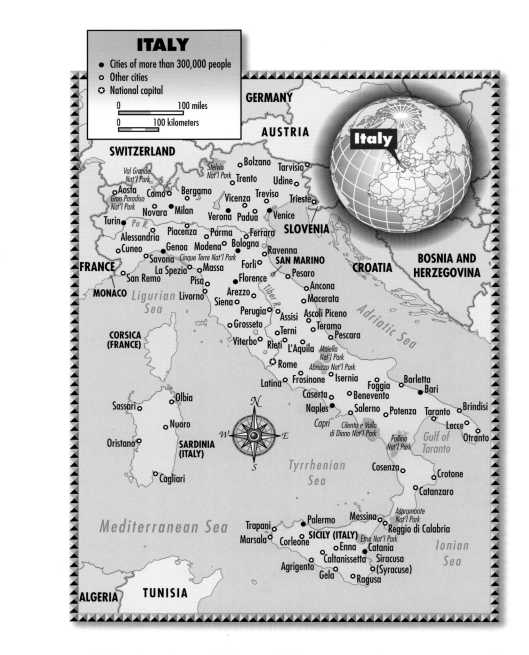

ITALY

- ● Cities of more than 300,000 people
- ○ Other cities
- ✪ National capital

0 ——— 100 miles
0 ——— 100 kilometers

GERMANY

AUSTRIA

SWITZERLAND

Val Grande
Nat'l Park

Stelvio
Nat'l Park

○Bolzano   Tarvisio○
○Trento
Udine

○Aosta
Gran Paradiso
Nat'l Park
○Como ○Bergamo
○Novara ●Milan
Vicenza○ Treviso○
Verona● Padua○
Trieste○
SLOVENIA

Turin○ Po R.

Alessandria○ Piacenza○ Parma○ Ferrara○
○Cuneo ○Genoa Modena● Bologna●
Savona○ Cinque Terre Nat'l Park ○Ravenna
La Spezia○ ○Massa Forlì○ SAN MARINO
San Remo○ Pisa○ Florence● ○Pesaro
MONACO Ligurian Sea Livorno○ ○Ancona
Arezzo○ ○Macerata
Siena○ Tiber R.
Perugia○ Ascoli Piceno○
CORSICA
(FRANCE) ○Assisi ○Teramo
Grosseto○ Terni○ ○Pescara
Viterbo○ Rieti○ L'Aquila○ Maiella
Nat'l Park
✪Rome Abruzzo Nat'l Park
Latina○ ○Frosinone ○Isernia
Foggia○ Barletta○
Sassari○ Caserta○ ○Benevento ●Bari
Naples● ○Salerno Brindisi○
Olbia○ ○Potenza Taranto○
Nuoro○ Capri Cilento e Vallo
di Diano Nat'l Park Lecce○
Oristano○ Pollino Otranto○
Nat'l Park Gulf of
Taranto
SARDINIA
(ITALY) Tyrrhenian
Sea Cosenza○ ○Crotone
Cagliari○ ○Catanzaro

FRANCE

Ligurian Sea

Adriatic Sea

CROATIA

BOSNIA AND
HERZEGOVINA

Mediterranean Sea

Aspromonte
Nat'l Park
Trapani○ ○Palermo Messina○
Marsala○ Reggio di Calabria○
SICILY (ITALY) Etna Nat'l Park
Corleone○ Enna○ Catania○
Caltanissetta○ Siracusa○
Agrigento○ (Syracuse)
Gela○ ○Ragusa

Ionian
Sea

Italy

School ends at 1:30 p.m. Roberto races home to eat with his parents and grandparents. They all live in the same apartment. On most days, they eat lunch together. Today, they have salad, ham, and pasta with tomato sauce.

After lunch, Roberto heads outside to play soccer with Gianni and other children. Running, kicking, and laughing, they quickly work up a sweat. Later, they walk to their favorite gelato shop. Gelato is Italian ice cream. It is bursting with flavor. Roberto gets *nocciola*, hazelnut. Gianni gets *flor di latte*, which is milk flavor. It's wonderfully creamy and perfectly sweet. After devouring their gelato, Roberto and Gianni stroll home, through quiet squares with fountains where old men sit chatting on benches. They pass historic churches filled with fantastic works of art, and go down busy streets, where buses, cars, and scooters fight for space. It's been another good day in Italy.

Soccer is the most popular sport in Italy. Children play it wherever there is space.

Gathering the People

Roberto is proud of his country's rich history. Two thousand years ago, Rome was the center of a vast empire that stretched across Europe and into Asia and Africa. The city is still scattered with the remains of ancient Roman buildings and monuments. After the Roman Empire fell apart in 476 CE, the region that is now Italy was occupied by a number of small kingdoms and city-states. Italy was not united as a single country until the 1800s.

Today, the country is divided into regions, which are a bit like U.S. states. A person's region may be important to him or her, but his or her own town is even more important. To many Italians, their hometown is the best possible place. Italians call this pride in where one is from *campanilismo*, from the word *campanile*, meaning "bell tower." Any person or place within sight, or at least sound, of the bells in a campanile has got to be the best. Italians can feel campanilismo even if their town has no actual bell tower.

Talking About Italy

A few phrases help explain Italians' love of life and their country. *La dolce vita*, for example, literally means "the sweet life." It expresses what many Italians want out of life: pleasure, relaxation, and happiness.

Another important phrase is *la bella figura*, meaning "the beautiful figure." Italians are generally conscious of wanting to show others a good image. This image extends to how they behave and how they dress. They always try to show their best side, their bella figura.

The phrase *Bel Paese*, meaning "beautiful country," refers to Italy itself. The term was originally used by the poet Dante Alighieri, who lived about seven hundred years ago.

British writer E. M. Forster said, "Love and understand the Italians, for the people are more marvelous than the land." Let's meet them.

Elderly men chat in Cortona, a city in central Italy.

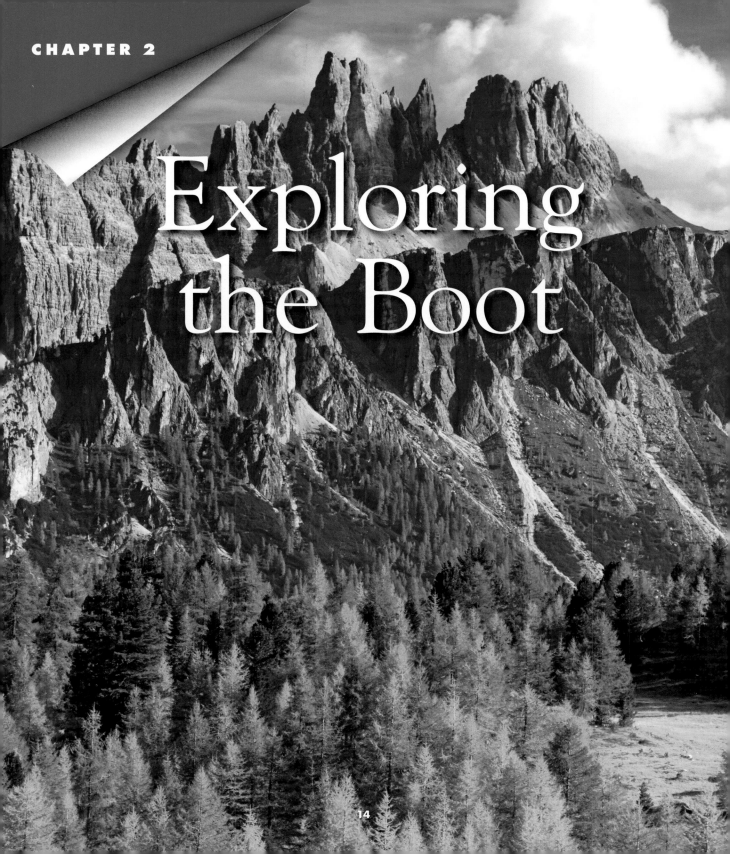

CHAPTER 2

Exploring the Boot

IT IS EASY TO RECOGNIZE ITALY ON A MAP. IT IS SHAPED like a tall, elegant boot with a flare at the top. Most of the boot sticks out southward from Europe into the Mediterranean Sea. East of the boot is the Adriatic Sea, and west is the Tyrrhenian Sea. These two seas are both arms of the Mediterranean. Altogether, Italy has about 4,700 miles (7,600 kilometers) of coastline, including dozens of islands.

France, Switzerland, Austria, and Slovenia all border Italy in the north. Italy also wraps completely around two tiny, independent states: Vatican City, the headquarters of the Roman Catholic Church, in the city of Rome; and the nation of San Marino, high in the Apennine Mountains in northern Italy.

Opposite: **The Dolomites are a mountain range in the Alps of northwestern Italy. They include eighteen peaks that rise above 10,000 feet (3,000 m).**

From North to South

The towering Alps stretch along Italy's northern border. They are the main mountain chain in Europe. The highest peak in Italy—and in all of Europe—is Mont Blanc ("White Mountain" in French), which lies along the border with France. It reaches 15,781 feet (4,810 meters) above sea level.

The height of the mountain changes a little bit every few years, because the summit is covered by a glacier—a giant sheet of ice. During warm years, the ice cap thins, and during colder years it gets thicker.

A climber crosses the snowy ice on Mont Blanc. The peak was first climbed in 1786.

Italy's Geographic Features

Area: 116,320 square miles (301,267 sq km)

Highest Elevation: Mont Blanc, 15,781 feet (4,810 m) above sea level

Lowest Elevation: Near Ferrara, 13 feet (4 m) below sea level

Longest River: Po River, 405 miles (652 km) long

Largest Lake: Lake Garda, 143 square miles (370 sq km)

Largest Island: Sicily, 9,925 square miles (25,705 sq km)

Coastline: About 4,700 miles (7,600 km), including islands

Highest Active Volcano: Mount Etna on Sicily, 11,053 feet (3,369 m) above sea level

Longest Shared Border: 460 miles (740 km), with Switzerland

Shortest Shared Border: 2 miles (3.2 km), with Vatican City

Greatest Distance North to South: 760 miles (1,223 km)

The Leaning Tower

One of the most famous landmarks in Italy is located in the town of Pisa, in Tuscany, a region of north-central Italy. It is a beautiful bell tower built near the Pisa Cathedral. Work began on the tower in the year 1173. It started leaning to the northwest even as it was being built because the soil beneath it was unstable. Work stopped for a century. When construction began again, the soil settled more, and the tower began to tilt to the north. Work stopped for another century, and the tower continued to shift. By the time construction started once more, the tower was leaning to the south. Over the centuries, architects tried many ways to stop the tower from tilting farther.

The tower was closed to the public in 1990 when a similar tower in the town of Pavia collapsed. In an effort to preserve the tower in Pisa, soil was moved from under the side that was too high. Cables were also placed around the tower to stabilize it, and the heavy bells atop the tower were removed. It was reopened to the public in 2001.

South of the mountains is the great Po Valley. The plain of the Po River is the country's largest agricultural region. It extends about 400 miles (645 km) from east to west.

In northwestern Italy, the land curves around the Ligurian Sea, forming the Italian Riviera. The city of Genoa lies in the center of this region, which is known for its picturesque villages, lovely landscapes, and mild weather. In the northeast, the land wraps around the Gulf of Venice, part of the Adriatic Sea. At the heart of this region is the city of Venice, which is located on 117 islands and has canals instead of streets. Venice was once one of the world's great trading cities.

The Apennine Mountains run the full length of Italy. They begin at the Alps and go almost to the Gulf of Taranto in the south. The highest point in the Apennines is Corno Grande in Abruzzo, about halfway down the peninsula. It rises about 9,554

The National Park of Abruzzo, Lazio, and Molise includes many Apennine peaks that rise above 7,000 feet (2,200 m).

San Marino

On a mountaintop in the Apennines between the provinces of Emilia-Romagna and Marche is the tiny nation of San Marino. The nation probably began as a monastery, where Catholic monks lived and worshipped, sometime around 301 CE. Today, about thirty-two thousand people live in San Marino. The nation occupies just 24 square miles (62 square kilometers) of land, making it one of the world's smallest nations. It is also one of the world's most prosperous nations, with much of its income from tourism and banking.

Vineyards cover the hillsides in the Tiber River valley. In 2010, Italy surpassed France to become the world's largest wine producer.

feet (2,912 m) high. A glacier located on the north side of the mountain is the most southerly glacier in Europe.

Rome, the capital of Italy, is located midway down the boot, along the Tiber River. Much of the Latium Plain, around the Tiber, is used for growing olives and wine grapes.

The land in Puglia is made of limestone rock, which erodes easily. This creates a rough, rugged landscape.

Southern Italy, including the islands of Sardinia and Sicily, is often called the Mezzogiorno. The name, meaning "midday sun," comes from the region's bright, hot summer sun. The whole of the south is very mountainous. The region called Puglia includes the heel of Italy's boot and has more flat land than most of southern Italy. Groves of olive trees, dense vineyards, and fields of grain lie within sight of the twinkling blue sea.

Islands

Sicily is the largest island in the Mediterranean Sea. It covers 9,925 square miles (25,705 sq km), making it slightly bigger than the U.S. state of Vermont. Sicily lies just across the narrow Strait of Messina from the mainland and looks something like a ball being kicked by the boot of Italy. Sicily is quite mountainous. The highest peak is Mount Etna, Europe's most active volcano. Five million people live on the island of Sicily. The largest city is Palermo, on the northwestern coast.

Much of the coast of Sardinia is rocky. The point at Capo Testa is covered with boulders.

Farther north is Sardinia, the second-largest island in the Mediterranean. Sardinia is only slightly smaller than Sicily, but it has a much smaller population. Only about 1.6 million people live there. The largest city on Sardinia is Cagliari.

Off the coast of Tuscany in the Tyrrhenian Sea is a chain of islands called the Tuscan Archipelago. These islands have become popular resort areas. The largest island in the chain, and the third-largest island in Italy, is Elba. Tuscan Archipelago National Park protects these islands and the ocean habitats around them.

Italy also controls some islands in the Adriatic Sea, off its east coast. The Tremiti Islands lie near Puglia. The name, which means "tremors," refers to the area's many earthquakes.

The Active Planet

The earth's outer layer is broken up into giant pieces called tectonic plates. These plates are constantly pushing against, pulling away from, and sliding past one another. Most volcanic eruptions and earthquakes occur along the boundaries between these plates.

Southern Italy lies atop the border between the African and the Eurasian Plates, and Italy is home to most of the active volcanoes in Europe. Mount Etna on Sicily is the tallest volcano in Europe. It is also one of the most active volcanoes in the world, frequently spewing ash and fountains of lava from its snowy summit. Other volcanoes in Italy include Vesuvius,

Lava spews from one of the four major craters on top of Mount Etna.

Buried Alive

In 79 CE, Mount Vesuvius exploded with a massive eruption. Hot ash, stone, and gas smothered the cities of Pompeii and Herculaneum (right), resort towns where the elite among the ancient Romans went to enjoy the seaside. About sixteen thousand people died in the eruptions. These historic cities were not rediscovered until 1748. Since then, most of the buildings and many skeletons have been uncovered.

on the mainland near Naples, and Stromboli, in the Aeolian Islands north of Sicily. Long ago, other volcanoes that are now dormant created many of Italy's islands and hills.

Predicting Earthquakes

Small earthquakes and tremors have often shaken L'Aquila, a city in central Italy, in the region of Abruzzo. In early April 2009, the area felt many tremors, but several officials said that a full earthquake was "unlikely." On April 6, a major quake struck, killing 287 people and destroying many historic buildings in the city. Six scientists and one government official were charged with involuntary manslaughter because they had failed to predict the strong earthquake and because, the prosecutors said, they had been "falsely reassuring." In 2012, the seven were found guilty and sentenced to six years in prison. Scientists around the world were appalled. Earthquakes cannot be predicted with accuracy. Some Italian scientists employed in key safety positions resigned because of this verdict. They feared that they, too, could be charged with a crime should disaster strike.

Italy has also experienced earthquakes. Most, but far from all, have taken place in the southern part of the country. The worst earthquake in Italy's recorded history occurred at Messina on Sicily in 1908. Tens of thousands of people died.

Children play in the snow in Milan, a city in northern Italy. On average, it snows seven days a year in Milan.

Climate

Italy has a wide range of climates to go along with its wide range of landscapes. High in the Alps, where no trees grow, is an alpine climate. This area is cold and snowy.

The Apennine Mountains block the winds that blow across Italy from the northeast. This means that the east side of the mountains experiences cold winds, while the west side is warmer and rainier. On the west side, temperatures are more moderate in both winter and summer.

The Po Valley, which cuts across northern Italy, has long, cold winters. Summers there are hot and humid. Southern Italy has hot, dry summers and mild winters. This weather draws visitors to the region's many beaches.

People walk through the streets of Erice, Sicily. Winters in southern Italy are frequently damp.

A Look at Italian Cities

Rome is the capital of Italy and its largest city, with an estimated population of 3,357,000 in 2012, but the nation also has many other vibrant cities.

Milan, Italy's second-largest city, with an estimated population of 2,962,000, is the nation's commercial and industrial capital. It is also a fashion capital of the world. Armani, Versace, Missoni, and Prada are among the design houses located there. The city's main square is the Piazza del Duomo. Many important buildings line the square, including the Milan Cathedral (below), the largest church in Italy.

Naples (right), the nation's third-largest city, is home to about 2,270,000 people. It is an important world port. Only Hong Kong, China, has more people passing through its port each year. Naples was originally settled by the Greeks three thousand years ago. Today, the city is filled with historic buildings. The hulking Castel Nuovo

(New Castle), which dates from the 1200s, overlooks the bay. Hundreds of historic churches line the city's narrow streets. Among the most important are the Cathedral of Naples and the Church of Santa Chiara.

Turin is Italy's fourth-largest city, with a population of about 1,662,000. The city was the center of activity leading to the unification of Italy and it served as the capital of the new country from 1861 to 1865. Like Milan, it is now an industrial and business city. It is the center of Italy's manufacturing industries, particularly of automobiles. The city is famous for the Shroud of Turin, a piece of linen that many people believe once covered the body of Christ. It is on display at San Giovanni Battista Cathedral.

CHAPTER 3

Natural Italy

ITALY IS RICH IN WILDLIFE. BECAUSE THE ITALIAN Peninsula juts out into the Mediterranean Sea, more species live in or migrate through Italy than any other European country. Italy serves as a pathway for animals passing through from Africa, central and northern Europe, and the Middle East. More than fifty-seven thousand animal species have been identified in Italy. About half of all European plant species are found in Italy, and many of them grow only in this country.

Mammals

Italy's largest mammals live in the sea. Whales and dolphins swim in the Ligurian Sea off Italy's northwestern coast.

The Apennine, or Marsican, brown bear is the largest land mammal in Italy, but it is very rare. One of the few places this bear lives is in Abruzzo National Park, east of Rome. It is estimated that the number of Apennine brown bears in the park may be so small that the bears might not survive. Conservationists have reintroduced Apennine brown bears

The horns on mouflons average about 25 inches (63 cm) long.

into the Dolomite Mountains of northern Italy, however. About fifty bears are now thriving in that region.

The mouflon, or wild sheep, is known for its big curved horns. It lives in the mountains of Campania, in southern Italy. Related to the mouflon is the alpine ibex, a wild goat that lives high in the mountains. It has shorter, less curving horns than the mouflon. By the nineteenth century, this ibex had disappeared from most of Europe. It lived only in Gran Paradiso National Park, in northern Italy. The population had declined to just 104 in 1976, before they were protected. The population has now rebounded, and there are tens of thousands of ibex living throughout the Alps.

The national animal of Italy is the Italian wolf. It is a subspecies of the common gray wolf. It is also called the Apennine wolf because it lives primarily in the Apennine Mountains. Italian wolves hunt at night, preying on such animals as deer, boars, and rabbits. If they get too close to where humans live, they may prey on livestock or ransack garbage. Wolves also eat berries and other plant parts. Italian wolves are officially protected. The number of wolves in Italy was at its lowest point in the 1970s. It has since been steadily increasing. Today, there are an estimated five hundred to seven hundred wolves in Italy.

Italy has several species of deer, including the roe deer and red deer. Though Italian deer, like those in other parts of the world, generally prefer forested areas, they often venture into suburban gardens. They also like the young shoots on grape plants in vineyards.

Wild boars are also drawn to vegetable gardens. These wild pigs weigh on average about 220 pounds (100 kilograms).

Birds

At least 525 species of birds either live in Italy or pass through it during migration. Coastal areas attract seabirds such as albatrosses, divers, and storm petrels. Storks fly over Italy on their way from Africa to countries farther north. Inland, waterfowl are plentiful. Pink flamingos live in the Po Valley near salty lakes, where they feed on shrimp and algae. These lakes also draw spoonbills, stilts, herons, egrets, and terns.

One of the most distinctive birds to spend time in Italy is the hoopoe. It has a large peaked crest on its tannish-pink head, and its back half is striped black and white. The hoopoe is becoming rare in much of Europe, but Italy still has a large population of this bird.

Plant Life

Nearly 6,800 types of plants grow in Italy. At least seven hundred plant species grow nowhere else in the world. Evergreen trees are common in the Alps, while oaks and chestnuts grow in the mountains of southern Italy. In the foothills, cork oaks and Aleppo pines are common, and sea grape trees grow on dunes along the coast.

Italy is known for its many olive trees, both planted and wild. Olives can be either shrubs or trees. They have silvery green leaves and small white flowers that turn into the fruit enjoyed by people the world over. Old olive trees develop thick gnarled trunks. One olive tree in Sardinia is estimated to be three thousand years old.

National Parks

Italy has twenty-four national parks. The first, Gran Paradiso National Park, was established in 1922. Lying in the north-west of the country, it includes high mountain peaks and abundant wildlife, including the wild ibex. In 2011, a bearded vulture baby hatched in the park. It was the first one born in the wild in the western Italian Alps in almost a century.

Olive trees are very hardy. They can live more than a thousand years, and their trunks continue to grow the entire time.

Farther east is Val Grande National Park. It lies along the shores of Lake Maggiore, Italy's second-largest lake. Val Grande is the largest wilderness area in Italy. In the past, shepherds took their herds up into the high mountains of this region for the summer. Since this way of life is no longer common, much of the land is returning to its natural state.

The most unusual Italian national park is also the smallest. Cinque Terre National Park is located on the Ligurian coast in northern Italy. It consists of five small towns built on cliffs above the sea. Its biggest dangers are too many tourists and the

Manarola is one of the five villages of the Cinque Terre. It was founded in the twelfth century.

The Bosnian pine tree is the symbol of Pollino National Park.

possibility of landslides. Two of the towns came close to being completely destroyed in several days of heavy rain in 2011.

Pollino National Park is the largest of Italy's national parks. The park is located in an isolated part of southern Italy and gets few visitors. The park is home to a major stand of the rare Bosnian pine tree. Italy's second-largest national park is also in southern Italy. Aspromonte National Park is home to the threatened Bonelli's eagle and many Italian wolves.

Etna National Park protects the area around Mount Etna on Sicily. The volcano is erupting almost continuously. Lava often shoots up from Etna's craters or breaks through the mountain slopes. The land on the lava slopes is very fertile. Much of it is covered with forests.

The Sinking City

The city of Venice has been slowly sinking ever since its construction began 1,600 years ago. Venice was built on islands. It has canals rather than streets and boats rather than cars. The first floor of many of the palaces built along its canals became unusable long ago as the buildings sank and the waves ate away at the buildings. In the twentieth century, matters became worse

when the city sank another 11 inches (28 centimeters). Frequently, heavy rains or high seas flood the city's public squares, including the plaza outside St. Mark's Basilica (above), the largest church in the city and a major tourist attraction. Boards are set up so people can walk across the flooded square. Since 2003, Italy has been working on a system to protect the city from such water damage. It consists of seventy-eight giant metal plates anchored in the seabed. When high water is predicted, the plates will be raised, blocking the waters from flooding the city. The project is expected to be completed in 2014.

Environmental Problems

Italy struggles to balance the need for a cleaner environment with the need to create jobs for people. In 2012, a court ordered the largest steel plant in Europe, located in the southern city of Taranto, to shut down because toxic emissions from the plant had caused serious illnesses in the region. Because the plant employs twelve thousand workers, the government is trying to find a way to keep it open while it cleans up its act.

In recent years, Italy has begun to focus more on environmental protection. Many cities, such as Bologna, which have long had problems with air pollution, have limited the use of private cars in the city center. Many Italians are now realizing that they must tackle water pollution, especially from factories, with the same energy that they have tackled air pollution. In general, Italy's regions have been more active in dealing with environmental problems than the national government has.

Parts of central Bologna are closed to traffic.

CHAPTER 4

The Story of Italy

THE LONG, BOOT-SHAPED ITALIAN PENINSULA THAT juts into the Mediterranean Sea served as the gateway to Europe when early people began migrating out of Africa. The first people in what is now Italy hunted animals and gathered wild plants to survive. Gradually, people learned to plant crops. Farming the land gave people a steady food supply and enabled them to stay in one place. Eventually, they built houses, towns, and cities.

Opposite: **People of the Etruscan civilization carved these life-size winged horses in the fifth century BCE. The Etruscans lived in the area north of what is now Rome.**

Early Peoples

A people called the Umbri occupied the area around what is now Rome from about the ninth to the fourth centuries BCE. They built forts on hilltops and sacrificed animals to their gods. Their language is extinct, but Umbria, a region north of Rome, still bears their name.

People of Italy, 500 BCE

- Carthaginians
- Etruscans
- Umbri
- Greeks
- Latins
- Samnites
- —— Present-day Italy

West of Umbria, in the land of Etruria, the Etruscan civilization flourished from about the eighth century to the third century BCE. The Etruscans were great traders, selling their crops and metals to the Greeks and the Carthaginians (in northern Africa). South of Umbria was a large group called the Samnites, who thrived from the sixth century to the third century BCE.

Starting around 800 BCE, many Greeks settled in Italy. They built great temples and bridges, especially in the south. Many magnificent Greek structures remain today.

Paestum was a Greek city located about 50 miles (80 km) southeast of what is now Naples. The ruins of several magnificent temples still stand there.

The Birth of Rome

The ancient Romans believed that their civilization was started in 753 BCE by twin brothers, the sons of the god Mars and a priestess. The infant boys, Romulus and Remus, were abandoned in the Tiber River. They landed onshore, where a female wolf found them and fed them. A shepherd and his wife raised them until, as adults, they founded a town at the place where the wolf had found them. That is said to have been on the Palatine Hill, which now lies in the center of Rome.

The Latin people moved to the Italian boot from farther north, starting around the eighth century BCE. They moved into Latium, the area around Rome, and gradually built the mighty Roman Empire. They conquered many of the neighboring groups, including the Etruscans and the Samnites in the third century BCE. Rome, the central city of the Latin people, was the first city in the world to have a million inhabitants.

From Republic to Empire

Rome was thriving. By about 509 BCE, it had become a republic, a form of government in which the leader is chosen, rather than being a monarch who inherits the title. In ancient Rome, the leading citizens voted for a senate, which ran the republic. Common people and slaves made up the majority of the population. They had no vote.

Early Rome's most frequent enemy was Carthage, a city-state in North Africa. For more than a hundred years the two states fought in a series of wars called the Punic Wars. In

Roman Empire

- Roman Empire, 264 BCE
- Added by 146 BCE
- Added by 44 BCE
- Added by 14 CE
- Added by 117 CE
- Temporary gain
- —— Present-day Italy

one of the wars, Carthaginian general Hannibal led a surprise attack on Rome by marching with war elephants through the snow-covered Alps. Rome finally destroyed Carthage in 146 BCE.

Rome quickly expanded the territory under its control, both through treaties and through the might of the Roman army.

Julius Caesar was one of Rome's greatest generals. Caesar was a brilliant military leader and organizer. He grew increasingly powerful, and by 49 BCE had become the dictator of Rome. Other Roman leaders opposed his claim to power and had him assassinated in 44 BCE.

Thirteen years later, in 31 BCE, Caesar's grandnephew and adopted son, Octavian, created the Roman Empire. In 27 BCE, he became known as Augustus, the "sacred one."

By about 200 CE, the Roman Empire reached its greatest extent, stretching over at least 2.2 million square miles (5.7 million sq km). Roman territory reached north to Great Britain, east into Syria, and south into Egypt. Within that territory lived about one-fourth of the world's people.

The Fall of the Empire

The Roman Empire lasted about five hundred years. Over the years, fighting among the leaders as well as attacks from the outside tore the empire apart.

Emperor Diocletian split the empire into two parts in 293 CE. Soon, the leader of the eastern section, Constantine, became powerful enough to take over the whole empire. He became a Christian and turned the empire into a Christian state. His capital was not Rome but Byzantium, in what is now Turkey. He renamed the city Constantinople (today it is Istanbul).

The weak Western Roman Empire was frequently invaded from the north by Germanic tribes, such as the Huns and the Vandals. The empire fell in 476 when a German chieftain threw out the last emperor, Romulus Augustulus.

Mysterious Cleopatra

In 48 BCE, Julius Caesar went to Egypt, where he met and fell in love with Cleopatra, the queen of Egypt. When he returned to Rome, she followed him, bringing along a son she claimed was his. The Roman people were appalled yet fascinated by her. When Caesar was assassinated, Cleopatra returned to Egypt. Only a short time later, Mark Antony, who had been Caesar's second-in-command, went to Egypt. He, too, fell in love with Cleopatra.

Back in Rome, Augustus, the emperor, became certain that Mark Antony and Cleopatra together were trying to establish an empire that would surpass Rome. He declared war on Mark Antony. Egyptian and Roman forces met in a battle off the coast of Actium in Greece in 31 BCE. The Egyptians, seeing they were losing the battle, withdrew. The Romans followed Cleopatra and Mark Antony to Egypt, where the two committed suicide to avoid being taken by Roman forces.

During the following century, the region was wracked by war. Tribal people flowed in from the north. Among them were a Germanic people called the Lombards. They formed a new kingdom that occupied much of the peninsula. The Lombards did not add on to the cities of the Roman Empire. Instead, they let the cities deteriorate. The Lombards lived in small, fortified settlements. They gradually gave up their belief in many gods and joined the Byzantine Catholic Church.

In 774, troops of King Charlemagne, the king of the Germanic people called Franks, captured Lombardy. In response, the pope, the head of the Roman Catholic Church, gave Charlemagne the title of Holy Roman emperor. German kings used this title for the next thousand years.

Changing Power and Wealth

In the centuries after the fall of the Roman Empire, different areas of the Italian Peninsula rose and fell in importance. This time is known as the medieval period, or Middle Ages (between the ancient world and the modern world).

From the sixth century, Rome and the area around it had been an independent Papal State, meaning it was under the control of the pope, the head of the Roman Catholic Church. Over the years, the Papal States grew through conquest and politics. The popes built this land into a powerful nation. At various times these states included the regions known today as Emilia-Romagna, Marche, Umbria, and Lazio.

During this period, many parts of Italy were city-states. These were small independent states that consisted of a city and the countryside around it. Italian city-states included Venice, Genoa, Verona, Florence, and many others. Venice, in northeastern Italy, became a hugely successful city-state and military power. The Venetians controlled shipping throughout much of the world.

Not all of Italy was divided into city-states. Lombardy's power spread across northern Italy. Neighboring Piedmont belonged to the French. The duke who ruled Piedmont extended his power over Sardinia, resulting in the Kingdom of Sardinia. This kingdom existed on and off until the nineteenth century. In the south, Arabs from Africa conquered and held Sicily for a hundred years, until the Normans, people of Norse and Viking descent who controlled northern France, took it away. The mainland of southern Italy was Greek territory, as it had been since about 250 BCE. Eventually, the

Italian City-States, 1500

Kingdom of Sicily, which was controlled by the Normans, came to rule most of this region. Later, Sicily pulled out of that kingdom. What remained became the Kingdom of Naples, which was still controlled by the French.

The Italian people carried on with their lives, without paying much attention to who controlled them politically. The seasons and the church ordered their lives. Latin was the most common written language, both because it was the language left over from the Roman Empire and because the Catholic Church used it.

Venice grew to be a wealthy and powerful city in the Middle Ages. It controlled much of the trade between Europe and Asia.

Marco Polo, the son of a great Venetian merchant family, traveled with his father and uncle to trade in the Mongol Empire of Asia. Kublai Khan was emperor when the Polo family arrived. Marco Polo spent more than twenty-five years in the courts of the Khans, sometimes as an employee, sometimes as a prisoner. He and his family were finally allowed to go home in 1292. Marco Polo wrote about his time in Asia, the places he had seen, and the people he had met. His popular writing gave many Europeans their first glimpse of the Far East.

The Renaissance

Florence, a city in Tuscany, became one of the great cities of the world during the Middle Ages. Its wealth was based on the wool trade. But the medieval period would soon end in a flourish of literature, art, and exploration. This period would come to be called the Renaissance, which means "rebirth." The name refers to a rebirth of the artistic traditions of ancient Greece and Rome.

One of the first signs of this rebirth was the writing of a poet named Dante Alighieri, who lived in Florence in the early fourteenth century. Dante did not write in Latin. Instead, he wrote his epic poem *The Divine Comedy* in the Tuscan language. Eventually, the popularity of his writing helped make Tuscan the language of almost everyone on the peninsula. It evolved into what is known today as Italian.

Florence and many other Italian cities had grown wealthy during this period. Prominent families and the pope used some of their wealth to pay artists and architects to make outstanding buildings and art. Chief among these wealthy families were the Medicis, who ruled Florence for several hundred years. They paid for work by sculptor and painter Michelangelo Buonarroti, painter and scientist Leonardo da

Michelangelo Buonarroti sculpted this statue of Lorenzo de' Medici for his tomb in Florence.

Father of Modern Science

Science flourished during the Renaissance. Astronomer Galileo Galilei (1564–1642), who was born in Pisa, near Florence, is sometimes called the Father of Modern Science. After learning about the Dutch invention of the telescope in 1608, Galileo built his own the following year. He used it to discover that there was more to the universe than people could see. He soon discovered the four largest moons of the planet Jupiter. Further observations led him to the conclusion that the earth moves around the sun. The official position of the Roman Catholic Church was that the earth was at the center of the universe and did not move. Galileo was eventually found guilty of heresy, which is disagreeing with an official opinion of the church. He was imprisoned in his home for the rest of his life, but he continued his scientific work. In 1992, the Roman Catholic Church acknowledged that it had been wrong, and Galileo had been right.

Vinci, architect Filippo Brunelleschi, philosopher Niccolò Machiavelli, and many others. Some of the work paid for by the Medicis still draws tourists to Florence and Rome today.

Changing Times

The Renaissance was already coming to an end in Italy by about 1550, although it later blossomed in other countries. Also coming to an end was the independence of most city-states. Many different states began vying for control over different parts of Italy. In 1527, Rome was attacked by troops of Holy Roman emperor Charles V.

Giuseppe Garibaldi spent twelve years in South America, where he learned military tactics and supported independence movements.

For almost three hundred years, Italy remained in the hands of outsiders—Spain, Austria, and France. By 1799, the French, under Napoléon Bonaparte, controlled much of the peninsula. After Napoléon was removed from power in 1814, European leaders meeting at the Congress of Vienna divided most of Italy among Austria, the Kingdom of Sardinia, the Kingdom of the Two Sicilies (Naples and Sicily), the Papal States, and Tuscany. A new time, called the *Risorgimento* or "resurgence," began.

Unifying Italy

In the years after Napoléon's defeat, nationalism grew across the Italian Peninsula. The Austrian Empire, which took over most of northern Italy, fought that nationalism on the Italian Peninsula. The French protected the Papal States. But the movement to become a nation grew. Italians, led by a man named Giuseppe Garibaldi, fought Austrian troops in many battles.

Garibaldi believed that Italians should be unified and free. Those beliefs forced him into exile in South America, where he learned to fight. He returned to Italy in 1848 to fight for independence but soon was forced to retreat. In 1859, a larger fight for freedom began in Italy. Garibaldi formed an army and began winning battles in the north. In 1860, he led a thousand of his followers to Sicily and soon claimed the island. Garibaldi and his men moved on to Calabria on the mainland and soon entered Naples. After this, the Kingdom of the Two Sicilies voted to be part of the Kingdom of Sardinia, which was based in Piedmont, in northern Italy. Within months, the expanded Kingdom of Sardinia became the core of the new unified Kingdom of Italy.

Some Italians wanted to build a republic. Others wanted to keep a monarchy. The monarchists prevailed, and Victor Emmanuel II, king of Sardinia, became king of the new

Giuseppe Garibaldi and his troops took control of Palermo, Sicily, in May 1860.

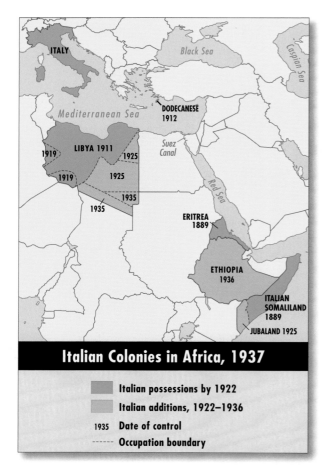

Italian Colonies in Africa, 1937

Italian possessions by 1922
Italian additions, 1922–1936
1935 Date of control
----- Occupation boundary

Kingdom of Italy in 1861. The Count of Cavour, an important supporter of the unification movement, became the first prime minister. The first parliament met on March 17, 1861, the date now celebrated as Unification Day.

The Italian Empire

The lives of the people living in unified Italy did not immediately improve. Some Italians wanted their country to be powerful once again, as it had been during the Roman Empire. They were heartened when the Suez Canal, connecting the Mediterranean Sea and the Red Sea, opened in 1869. The canal would help Italy compete with other European nations that were building overseas empires, because it made it easier for Italians to reach East Africa. Italy soon claimed Somaliland and Eritrea in eastern Africa. Italy tried to gain control of Ethiopia, too, but Ethiopian troops held off the Italian forces. In 1911, Italians managed to take Libya, in North Africa. And in 1936, Italy finally captured Ethiopia.

In World War I, Italy fought on the same side as the United Kingdom, France, Russia, and the United States against Germany and Austria-Hungary. At the war's end, Italy gained additional land in the northeast, near Austria. But the nation paid a high price. A half million Italians died in the war.

Benito Mussolini gave dramatic speeches that captured the attention of the crowds who gathered to hear him.

Mussolini and World War II

Italy was in crisis at the end of World War I. The economy was failing, and some people wanted Italy to become communist, meaning that the government would own the businesses and control the economy. Those who opposed that idea followed Benito Mussolini, who became the leader of the National Fascist Party. He became prime minister in 1922 and dictator soon after. The Fascists believed in intense nationalism, expanding their nation's territory, and strong leaders.

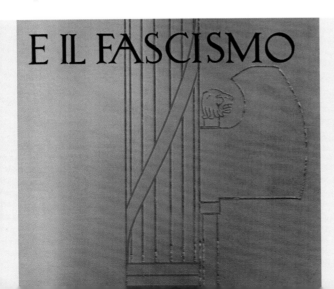

E IL FASCISMO

Fascism

The word *fascist* comes from an ancient Roman term for a bundle of birch rods (called a fasces) that was used as a symbol of power in the ancient Roman Republic. Benito Mussolini used that symbol because he thought it showed that the new Italians were an ancient, powerful people who were rising again under his dictatorship.

In the 1930s, in neighboring Germany, Adolf Hitler came to power as another Fascist dictator. Hitler and Mussolini began cooperating with each other. World War II began in 1939 when Germany invaded Poland. The following year, Italy entered the war on Germany's side, fighting the Allies—the United Kingdom, France, the Soviet Union, and eventually the United States. Japan later became part of the German-Italian alliance, called the Axis.

The Allies bombed Rome on May 16, 1943. They soon invaded Sicily and the far south of the mainland. The Allied troops thought they would be able to move quickly up the Italian Peninsula, but it took almost two years.

Italian king Victor Emmanuel III signed a peace agreement between the Allies and Italy in September 1943. He recognized that Mussolini's friendship with Hitler had come close to destroying Italy. Mussolini was removed from power and put in jail. German troops moved south to take control of central and northern Italy. Some Italians stationed nearby began to actively fight the Germans. They became a resistance movement.

The Italian Resistance

Many Italians joined the resistance. The members of the resistance, called partisans, made the war increasingly difficult for Germans. Brave men and women worked as couriers, sneaking secret messages to active partisans. They seized weapons whenever they could. They bombed German installations. Many died for their efforts. Almost forty-five thousand Italian partisans were killed during the war.

Some Germans helped Mussolini escape from prison and reach the north, where he established a government that was really controlled by Germany. He called it the Italian Social Republic. This government ended on April 25, 1945, when Allied troops, helped by Italian resistance fighters, pushed the Germans out of Italy. Mussolini was caught trying to flee and was killed. Germany surrendered the following month.

Allied forces invaded Sicily in July 1943, and by August they had captured the island.

The New Republic

After the war, the Italian people voted to make Italy a republic instead of a monarchy. For the first time, women voted along with the men. The first prime minister was Alcide De Gasperi of the Christian Democratic Party. That party remained in power for almost fifty years.

Italy was primarily an agricultural country until after World War II. Then, major industries helped the country's economy expand so quickly that this event was called *Il Miracolo* (the miracle). Millions of people moved from the poor regions of the south to the industrial north and other European countries where work was more plentiful. For a time, Italy was second only to Japan as the world's fastest expanding economy. In 1957, Italy was one of the six founding member nations of the European Economic Community (EEC). This organization wanted to improve economic cooperation among European nations.

Cars move through a Fiat factory in 1966. Fiat has been the biggest car manufacturer in Italy since 1910.

Members of the Red Brigades sit in jail. In the 1970s and early 1980s, the Red Brigades killed seventy-five people, including Italian prime minister Aldo Moro in 1978.

Terror and Corruption

Social and political unrest increased in the 1960s and 1970s. A communist group called the Red Brigades wanted to overthrow the Italian government. Its members used terrorist actions such as bombings, kidnappings, and murders to try to achieve this. They succeeded in making Italy less stable.

Meanwhile, organized crime groups called the Mafia were becoming more involved in politics and taking control of some towns. Political corruption also became common. Many politicians took bribes or enriched themselves through government activity. In the 1990s, Operation Clean Hands, a criminal investigation looking into government corruption, resulted in the arrest of more than seven hundred people.

The Mafia

In Sicily during the nineteenth century, a gang of criminals gained control of illegal activities in many towns. They developed a strict code of conduct and called themselves *Cosa Nostra*, meaning "our thing." Usually they are called the Mafia. No one knows for sure where the word came from, but it is often said to mean "swagger."

Members of the Mafia got involved in politics, first in Sicily and then throughout southern Italy. They tried to elect only people who would not try to prevent their crimes. This allowed the power of the Mafia to spread.

Silvio Berlusconi served as prime minister of Italy three times. He is also one of the wealthiest people in the world. He made a fortune from owning Italian television channels.

Recent Times

In 1993, the European Union (EU) was formed. The EU built on what the EEC had started. People can move freely among the member states. The EU allows free trade among its nations. This means that no taxes are collected when goods produced in one member country are sent to another member country. Twenty-seven European nations now belong to the EU. Seventeen of them, including Italy, use a common currency, called the euro.

Italy began using the euro in 2002, and for a time it prospered. But the nation was borrowing more money than it could easily pay back. This became a crisis when a worldwide economic downturn began in 2008. As the economy faltered, many Italians, particularly in the south, lost their jobs.

Silvio Berlusconi, a billionaire from the communications industry, served as prime minister three different times between 1994 and 2011. The nation's economic problems finally proved too great for Berlusconi to handle, and he was forced out of office. These economic problems will be one of the main challenges faced by Italy and the EU as a whole in the years to come.

In 2012, students protested cuts to Italy's education budget during the nation's financial crisis.

CHAPTER 5

Governing the Republic

ITALY IS A REPUBLIC, MEANING THAT THE PEOPLE CONTROL the nation through the representatives they elect. It has been a republic since 1948, in the aftermath of World War II. Before that it was a monarchy. Like the government of the United States, the Italian government is divided into three parts, or branches: executive, legislative, and judicial.

Opposite: **The Chamber of Deputies meets in Palazzo Montecitorio. It was built in the 1600s as a place where the pope could hold public events.**

Voting

Italians can vote in some elections at age eighteen, but they cannot vote in Senate elections until they are twenty-five. Women voted for the first time in 1946. In the most recent Italian national election, voter turnout was the lowest it has been since the start of the republic—about 75 percent.

Italians don't vote for individual members of Parliament, Italy's lawmaking body. Instead, they vote for a political party, which puts forward a list of people who would serve if the party won. If a party cannot win a majority of the seats, it must find one or more other parties that will work with it. These groups of parties are called coalitions.

The Capital City

Rome, the capital of Italy, is often called the City of Seven Hills. The city government offices are on Capitoline Hill, and the president of Italy has an official residence on the Quirinal Hill. Rome is also a city of grand boulevards and narrow side streets. It is a bustling city, but one that is filled with historic churches and fountains. Many visitors make a wish when they toss coins into the Trevi Fountain. According to tradition, this means they will return to Rome one day.

Rome's rich history and abundant art draw tourists from around the world. Ruins of ancient Rome are scattered throughout the city. One of the most popular ancient sites is the Roman Forum (below, top left), a large square that was the site of many important government buildings in the ancient city. Visitors flock to places such as the Capitoline Museums, the Borghese Gallery, and the Church of Santa Maria Maggiore to see endless examples of Italy's historical art and architecture.

Rome is also a thriving modern-day city, home to almost 3.5 million people in the city and its suburbs. Residents can take public transportation to ocean beaches or to Leonardo da Vinci International Airport. An efficient subway, called the Metropolitana or Metro, and bus system run through the area.

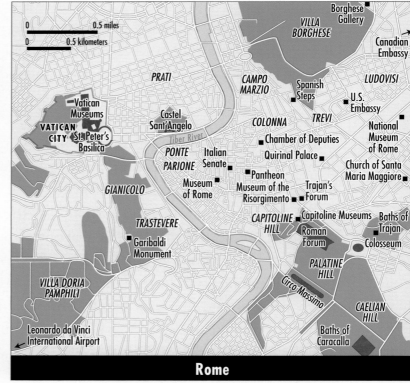

Legislative Branch

Italy's parliament has two houses. The lower house is the Chamber of Deputies. It meets in a seventeenth-century building called Palazzo Montecitorio. It has 630 seats, 12 of which are reserved for Italians living outside Italy. Members of the Chamber of Deputies must be at least twenty-five years old. They are elected to five-year terms, although the president can call for elections early.

Members of the Chamber of Deputies listen to Prime Minister Mario Monti speak in 2011.

The upper house of Parliament is the Senate. It meets in the Palazzo Madama, which was originally built for the Medici family. The Senate includes 315 seats for elected senators and several seats for people who are named senators for life because of their accomplishments. Senators have to be forty years old to run for office. Like deputies, elected senators serve terms of five years.

Executive Branch

The official head of the executive branch is the president, but this is primarily a ceremonial role. Members of Parliament elect the president, who lives in Quirinal Palace in Rome, to a seven-year term. The president names the prime minister, the person who actually runs the government. The president cannot choose just anyone, however, because the prime minister must have a majority of votes in both houses of Parliament.

The prime minister chooses a council of advisers, or cabinet, who are officially appointed by the president. The cabinet officers run the different departments of the government, such as justice, defense, health, and public works.

Sometimes the government loses the support of the majority coalition in Parliament. If the members vote that they have "no confidence" in the prime minister, then he or she

National Government of Italy

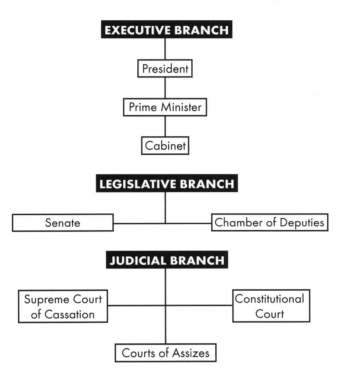

is forced to resign and a new prime minister is named. When this happens, the president can also call for new parliamentary elections. The Italian government has often been unstable. In the first fifty years after World War II, each government lasted on average only eleven months. Silvio Berlusconi, who controlled Italian politics for much of the period from 1994 to 2011, was forced to resign in November 2011. He was replaced temporarily by Mario Monti, an unelected prime minister. After the 2013 election, Enrico Letta was chosen to lead a coalition government. He faces the difficult task of trying to guide the country out of its economic problems.

Judicial Branch

The judicial branch of government has many levels. At the lowest level are local justices of the peace who handle simple noncriminal questions. Courts of Assizes try criminal cases. In both criminal and noncriminal cases, people can ask a district court to review a lower court decision. Both kinds of cases can also be taken to the Supreme Court of Cassation, the highest court, which has the power to overturn other courts' decisions.

A totally separate court called the Constitutional Court decides whether laws passed by Parliament are legal according to the constitution. It is made up of fifteen judges. Five of the

Judges on Italy's Constitutional Court deal with constitutional questions, charges against the president, and some conflicts between different parts of government.

The National Anthem

The lyrics of "Fratelli d'Italia" ("Brothers of Italy"), also known as "The Song of the Italians," was written by a young student named Goffredo Mameli in Genoa in 1847. The music was written by Michele Novaro. The song was popular during the struggle for unification, but it was not adopted as the national anthem until 1946.

Italian lyrics

Fratelli d'Italia
L'Italia s'è desta,
Dell'elmo di Scipio
S'è cinta la testa.
Dov'è la Vittoria?
Le porga la chioma,
Ché schiava di Roma
Iddio la creò

Stringiamoci a coorte
Siam pronti alla morte
Siam pronti alla morte
L'Italia chiamò.
Stringiamoci a coorte
Siam pronti alla morte
Siam pronti alla morte
L'Italia chiamò! (Sì!)

English translation

Brothers of Italy,
Italy has woken,
Bound Scipio's helmet
Upon her head.
Where is Victory?
Let her bow down,
For God created her
Slave of Rome.

Let us join in a cohort,
We are ready to die.
We are ready to die,
Italy has called.
Let us join in a cohort,
We are ready to die.
We are ready to die,
Italy has called! (Yes!)

judges are appointed by the president, another five are elected by Parliament, and the final five are elected by other court judges. The judges serve for nine years.

Police and Military

Italy has two major policing organizations. The first is the Carabinieri. It polices both civilians and the military. Unlike most national police forces, it also takes part in overseas peacekeeping duties. The second policing organization is the State Police. It includes those patrolling airports, highways, and railways. The State Police also assists the local police.

The Carabinieri is one of the four branches of the Italian military. The others are an army, a navy, and an air force. The military has been voluntary since 2003. More than three hundred thousand men and women served in the Italian military in 2011.

Regions

Italy is divided into twenty regions, which are similar to U.S. states. The largest region by area is Sicily. The largest by population is Lombardy. The smallest region by both area and population is Aosta Valley.

Regions

Five of the twenty regions have more power to govern themselves than the other regions do. Called autonomous (self-governing) regions, they are Friuli-Venezia Giulia, Sardinia, Sicily, Trentino–Alto Adige, and Aosta Valley. These regions keep more tax money than the other regions do, but in return they fund health care, schools, and other services. These autonomous regions are in areas with significant cultural differences from the rest of Italy.

Each region has an elected parliament and a president. In most regions, the people elect the president, but in Aosta Valley and Trentino–Alto Adige, a regional council chooses the president.

CHAPTER 6

Making a Living

TALY HAS ONE OF THE LARGEST ECONOMIES IN WESTERN Europe. It ranks fourth in the European Union in the total value of goods and services it produces, trailing only Germany, France, and Great Britain. But Italy still faces many challenges. It is poor in natural resources and has a limited amount of fertile land.

Farming the Land

Because Italy is so mountainous, much of the land is not suitable to agriculture. About 23 percent of Italian land is usable for agriculture, and another 31 percent is forest. About 4 percent of the Italian workers are employed in agriculture. This number has dropped dramatically in recent decades. In 1970, 20 percent of Italian workers were employed in agriculture.

The main growing region is the Po Valley. About one-third of all Italian cropland is used to grow grains. Durum, or "hard," wheat is the main grain crop in the south. It is the wheat that is used to make pasta. The next most common grains grown are corn and soft wheat. Soft wheat, used for bread and cake, is grown in the north. Although a lot of wheat is grown in Italy, the nation must still import more from other countries to keep up with the demand.

More rice is grown in Italy than any other European Union country. Most Italian rice is grown in Lombardy and Piedmont.

Olives are another major Italian agricultural product. The olive tree is native to the Mediterranean region. Since before recorded time, olives have been pressed to obtain oil that is used in cooking food and is burnt in small lamps to make light. Much of the trade carried on by early civilizations was in olive oil. Today, Italy is the second-largest producer of olive oil in the world, trailing only Spain.

Many other fruits are also grown in Italy. The country produces abundant peaches, pears, apricots, apples, and cherries.

Italians catch a huge amount of fish in both the Ligurian Sea and the Adriatic Sea. Fishing boats work out of at least eight hundred ports. The fishers sell about half the catch

Resources

Corn and wheat	Al	Aluminum	Mn	Manganese
Fruit and vegetables	Bx	Bauxite	Marb	Marble
Forests	C	Coal	NG	Natural gas
Grapes and wine	Cem	Cement		Oil
Livestock ranching	Clay	Clay	Pb	Lead
Nonagricultural land	Fe	Iron ore	Salt	Salt
	Feld	Feldspar	Zn	Zinc
	K	Potash		

What Italy Grows, Makes, and Mines

AGRICULTURE (2009)

Grapes	8,242,500 metric tons
Corn	7,877,700 metric tons
Wheat	6,341,000 metric tons

MANUFACTURING

Cars and trucks (2011)	790,348 units
Steel (2011)	28,700,000 metric tons
Chemicals (2010)	US$50,200,000,000 in sales

MINING

Natural gas (2011)	8,400,000,000 cubic meters
Petroleum (2010)	35,000,000 barrels
Feldspar (2010)	4,700,000 metric tons

directly to restaurants. Because fishing resources are shrinking, the European Union is trying to limit commercial fishing, especially in the Adriatic.

The Industrial Triangle

Three northern cities—Milan, Turin, and Genoa—form one of Europe's strongest industrial areas. This region, called the industrial triangle, is also the richest part of Italy. Milan is the industrial and business capital of Italy and one of the great economic centers of Europe. The Italian stock exchange and most of Italy's international banks are in Milan. Turin is the manufacturing heart of the nation. Genoa is its shipping center.

Making a Living **73**

Manufacturing

The largest privately owned company in Italy is Fiat, a car manufacturer. The name is an abbreviation of *Fabbrica Italiana Automobili Torino* (Italian Carmaker of Turin). The company was started in 1899. Since the 1950s, most cars on Italian highways have been Fiats. For a time, it was the biggest car manufacturer outside the United States. Today, it remains the biggest automaker in Italy. Fiats are built in factories around Turin. The world's largest iron foundry company, headquartered in Turin, also belongs to Fiat, as does *La Stampa*, an important Turin newspaper. Fiat employs a quarter of a million people, half of them in Italy. Many Fiats are also built in Brazil and Poland.

In recent decades, Fiat has bought up other car companies. It now owns the companies that make sports cars such as Alfa Romeos, Maseratis, and Ferraris. In 2009, Fiat bought part of the Chrysler Corporation in the United States. Its investment helped rescue Chrysler from being forced out of business.

Lamborghini, another sports car manufacturer, is based in Bologna. The company also owns Ducati, which produces what many people believe to be the best motorcycle in the world. Lamborghini is now owned by Audi, a German company. Piaggio, a company based in Tuscany, began making Vespa motor scooters in 1946, when people could not afford cars. In the following decades, Vespas and the similar Lambretta, made in Milan, became an important form of transportation for young people in Europe.

Steelmaking is another important industry in Italy and one that is growing rapidly. Italy supplies about 10 percent of the steel in the European market. In 2011, it produced about

Steel manufacturing is a major industry in Italy.

Women at Work

In Italy, about 68 percent of men between the ages of fifteen and sixty-four have jobs. But only 46.5 percent of Italian women work. In Europe, only Malta has a lower percentage of women in the workforce than Italy does. That is compared to 58.5 percent elsewhere in Europe and 59.2 percent in the United States.

Women are particularly underrepresented in powerful jobs. In 2012, women held only about 6 percent of the high-level positions in Italian business. That's one of the lowest rates in Europe. In response, Italy passed a law stating that, by 2015, women must make up 33 percent of each board of directors of all corporations. Companies that don't reach that number will be fined.

31.6 million tons (28.7 million metric tons), second only to Germany. Iron ore is used in making steel. Italy imports most of its iron ore from Brazil, in South America. A considerable amount also comes from Mauritania, a country in Africa.

Italy is a major manufacturer of appliances, electrical equipment, tools, and ships. The chemical industry is thriving in Italy, too.

Italy has long been known as a maker of high-quality textiles. The country produces silk, wool fabrics, and other types of cloth. Most textiles in Italy are now made on a large scale. But Italy also has a strong tradition of craftspeople. Generations of families have produced textiles, leather goods, jewelry, glasswork, and much more. Prada, one of the great clothing and leather companies in the world, started as a small leather goods shop owned by two brothers, Mario and Martino Prada,

Italy's Workforce (2011)

Services	67.8%
Industry	28.3%
Agriculture	3.9%

Italy is known for its high-quality textiles. Here, a man works a loom at a linen factory in Tuscany.

in Milan. Today, Mario's granddaughter Miuccia is the head designer at the company. Benetton, another worldwide clothing business, started in 1965 in Treviso when a young man sold his brother's bicycle in order to buy a knitting machine. He started making sweaters designed by his sister.

Into Space

Italy built the first satellite to be made by a country other than the United States or the Soviet Union (a country that separated into Russia and other neighboring nations in 1991). The *San Marco 1* was launched in 1964. Today, Italy is active in the European Space Agency, an organization that focuses on exploring and studying space. Astronaut Franco Malerba was the first Italian to fly to space, when he joined a U.S. space shuttle mission in 1992. Several Italian astronauts have spent long periods of time in the International Space Station, a research station that has been orbiting the earth since 1998. Italy's first woman astronaut, Samantha Cristoforetti, is expected to travel to the International Space Station in 2014.

The mountainous region of Trentino is on its way to becoming the "Silicon Valley of the Alps." Silicon Valley is an area of Northern California where many technology companies are located. Silicon Valley got its name because silicon is a material used in making computer parts. In recent years, many universities, nonprofit foundations, and private businesses have brought scientists to Trentino from other countries to develop research that will benefit Italy in the future. Companies from all over the world are establishing research centers there. The idea is paying off. Trentino has the highest average income of any area in Italy and the lowest unemployment.

Services

More than two-thirds of Italians work in service industries. These include fields such as banking, education, publishing, trade, and transportation. The service industry that employs the most workers in Italy is tourism. People who work in the tourist industry have jobs such as hotel clerk, waiter, salesperson, and tour guide.

A chef observes a student at a school for chocolate makers.

The Colosseum is one of Rome's most popular tourist sites. It is an outdoor stadium that was built during the Roman Empire two thousand years ago. It seated fifty thousand people, making it the largest stadium built by the Romans. Senators and priestesses sat around the outer edges of the arena floor, while slaves and women sat in the upper balconies.

Fighters called gladiators appeared in the arena to take part in armed combat. Some fought willingly, looking for glory. Others were slaves or persecuted Christians who were forced to fight to the death for the entertainment of the Roman elite. At various times, animals such as leopards, lions, elephants, giraffes, elks, and even rhinoceroses were released in the arena to be hunted by gladiators.

Over the centuries, the Colosseum deteriorated. One pope wanted to turn the Colosseum into a wool factory and add workshops and living quarters on the main and

upper floors. The hypogeum, the underground portion of the stadium, was filled with dirt and rubble for centuries. Archaeologists began to clean it out in the 1990s. One feature they uncovered was a winch that ancient Romans would turn to raise a cage bearing a lion or other animal to the main arena floor. In 2010, the hypogeum was opened to the public for tours.

Travelers have been coming to tour Italy for centuries. In the eighteenth and nineteenth centuries, educated Europeans were expected to explore the art and history of Italy. Today, about forty-five million foreign visitors travel to Italy each year. People still come for history and art, but they also enjoy the food, skiing, and gorgeous scenery.

Tourists fill the streets of San Gimignano, a small town in Tuscany. Italy is the fifth most visited country in the world.

Venice is the center of the art-glassmaking industry in Italy. For almost a thousand years, artisans have been making some of the world's finest glass objects on the Venetian island of Murano. The basic mineral used in making glass is sand. Murano has a supply of the highest quality quartz sand.

Mining

Italy's mineral resources are limited, but it does produce several important materials. It is the world's leading producer of feldspar, a material used in making glass and ceramics.

Another important resource found in Italy is marble, a smooth, hard rock that comes in many colors. Marble was an

A worker climbs a ladder at a marble quarry in Carrara, Tuscany. Marble has been mined in Carrara for thousands of years.

Many solar panels have been installed in Italy. In 2011, solar energy accounted for 3.6 percent of the nation's energy supply.

important building material in old Italy. Many buildings constructed during the Roman Empire were made of marble. Pure white marble is quarried at Carrara in Tuscany and has been used since ancient times for making statues. One of the most famous Renaissance statues made from this kind of marble is Michelangelo's *David*. It is on display in Florence.

Energy and the Environment

About 39 percent of the energy used in Italy comes from oil. Another 8 percent comes from coal. Italy produces a small amount of oil, but it imports much more. Although there is more oil available offshore under the Adriatic and Mediterranean Seas, many Italians are reluctant to let oil companies drill for it because they fear harmful oil spills.

Although Italy has the fifth-largest supply of natural gas in the European Union, it still must import most of the gas it needs. A pipeline is being built under the Mediterranean to carry natural gas from the African nation of Algeria to Italy.

Many Italians are eager to use renewable energy sources, which will never run out and do not emit harmful pollutants into the air. These sources include wind power, solar power, and moving water. About one-quarter of all electricity in Italy is produced by renewable resources. Most electricity made from the power of moving water is produced in the north, where there are more rivers than in the south. The largest hydroelectric dam in the country is Entracque in Valle Gesso, near the French border. Wind power accounts for about one-fifth of renewable energy in Italy. That amount is growing year by year. Solar power is also increasing. The nation's largest solar power station is at Montalto di Castro, west of Rome. It started producing electricity in late 2010.

Money Facts

Italy is one of seventeen countries in Europe that use the same currency called the euro. Italy replaced its old currency, the lira, with the euro in 2002. The symbol of the euro is €. In 2013, US$1.32 equaled €1, and €0.76 equaled US$1.

One euro is divided into one hundred cents. Coins are issued in values of 1, 2, 5, 10, 20, and 50 cents. There are also €1 and €2 coins. Bills, or banknotes, come in amounts of 5, 10, 20, 50, 100, 200, and 500 euros.

Each country in the Eurozone issues its own coins with a design of its choice on the front of the coin. Italian coins feature prominent images from Italian art and architecture. For example, the 5-cent coin shows the Colosseum in Rome. The reverse side of all euro coins shows a map of Europe. Banknotes are the same across the entire Eurozone. Each denomination has its own color. For example, the €100 bill is green, and the €200 bill is yellow. The front of each bill shows a window or a gateway, and the back shows a bridge.

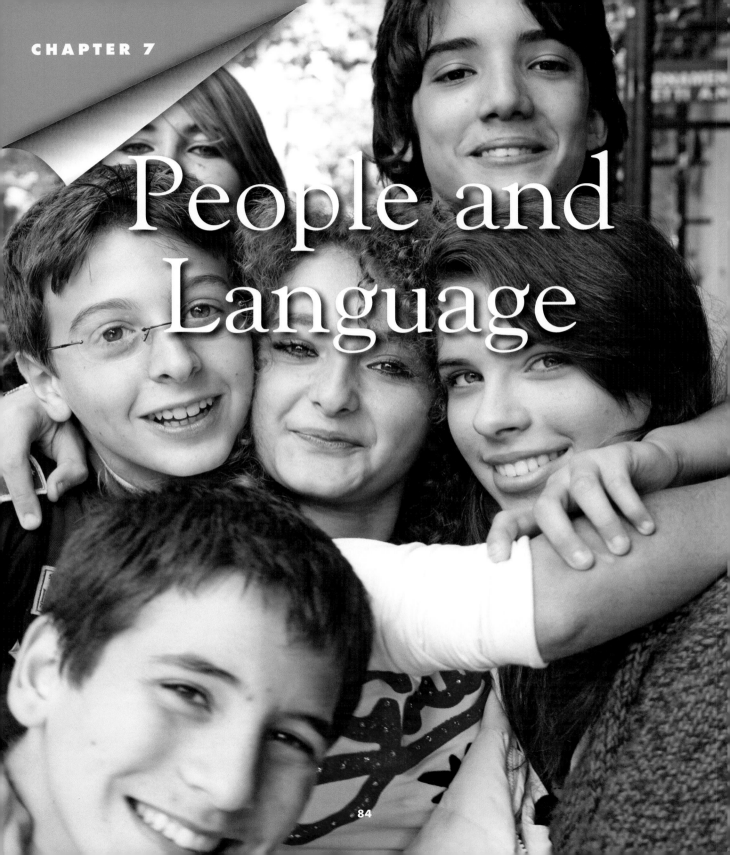

CHAPTER 7

People and Language

"**W**E HAVE MADE ITALY. NOW WE HAVE TO MAKE Italians." That's what an Italian politician said around the time of unification. To this day, the country has not completely succeeded in making a single people of all Italians. Each region has its own history, its own dialect, and its own customs.

In 2012, Italy had an estimated 61,261,254 residents. This made it the twenty-third largest country in population, though it is only seventy-second largest in area. It has a population density of 513 people per square mile (198 per sq km), making it one of the most densely packed countries in Europe.

Who Lives in Italy?

Most people who live in Italy are ethnically Italian. But there are German Italians, Slovene Italians, and Greek Italians living in border regions.

Opposite: **Teenagers hang out in Piazza Vanvitelli in Naples.**

An African immigrant sells bracelets in Milan. It is estimated that at least a million Africans have settled in Italy.

Ethnic Groups

Italian	95%
German	1%
French	1%
Albanian	1%
Slovenian	1%
Greek	1%

Europe's largest ethnic minority group is the Romani, who were formerly called Gypsies. About ten million Romani live in all of Europe, about 150,000 of them in Italy. The Romani originated in India. They began migrating around the world more than a thousand years ago, probably arriving in Europe by the early 1300s. Some Romani live as nomads, continually on the move. About 20 percent of Italian Romani are descended from people who settled on the Italian Peninsula six hundred years ago.

About 8 percent of the people who live in Italy are foreign residents. The largest group is from Romania, a country in eastern Europe. Many people from North Africa also live in Italy.

No matter where they come from, immigrants take the lowest paying jobs, as house cleaners or agricultural workers. Many immigrants think that they will stay in Italy for only a few years before returning home. However, once they start a life in Italy, with a job and a spouse and children, returning to their native country may not be so attractive. Immigrants cannot apply for citizenship until they have lived in Italy for ten years.

Population of Largest Cities (2012 est.)	
Rome	3,357,000
Milan	2,962,000
Naples	2,270,000
Turin	1,662,000
Palermo	872,000

Members of the Sikh religion attend a service in the town of Novellara, north of Bologna. Novellara has Europe's second-largest gurdwara, a Sikh place of worship.

Leaving Home

In years past, when Italy suffered economic trouble, many Italians decided to leave their homes behind and move to another country. From about 1890 to 1910, almost three million Italians immigrated to the United States. It is estimated that about 40 percent of them eventually returned to Italy. Still, the fourth-largest European ethnic group in the United States consists of people with Italian ancestry. Many Italians also immigrated to Brazil and Argentina in South America. In the years following World War II, thousands of Italians immigrated to Australia.

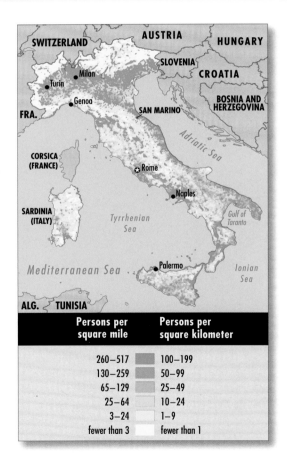

Persons per square mile		Persons per square kilometer	
260–517		100–199	
130–259		50–99	
65–129		25–49	
25–64		10–24	
3–24		1–9	
fewer than 3		fewer than 1	

Family

Family is important in Italy. Children often live with their parents until well past their thirtieth birthday. Four-fifths of all men between the ages of eighteen and thirty live with their parents. Young people are more likely to stay with their parents in the south, because jobs are more difficult to find there. In 2012, 25 percent of the young people were unemployed. Many can find only temporary jobs. They could not afford to live on their own even if they wanted to.

Although children are all-important to families, the number of children Italians are having has dropped dramatically in recent decades. From 1960 to 2010, Italy's birth rate dropped from 2.7 children per woman to 1.3. This gives Italy one of the lowest birth rates in the world. Italians are having so few children that the

nation's population is beginning to decline. This means that fewer young people are working and paying taxes to support increasing numbers of elderly people.

About one out of every five Italians is over age sixty-five. On average, Italian men live seventy-nine years and women live eighty-five years. Italians generally want to keep their elderly parents living with them, because they want to keep the family together. As a result, there are few retirement homes for elderly Italians. Sometimes, Italians hire women, particularly from eastern Europe, to take care of their parents. But often, Italians are taking care of their parents and their own children. One young man told a *Time* magazine reporter, "We keep Grandpa at home, but that means whoever takes care of him can't find a real job. You are always expected to be the good son of the family."

In Italy, it is common for several generations of one family to live together.

A chalkboard shows the menu for a restaurant in Tuscany. Most Italian words end in a vowel.

The Italian Language

Italian is called a Romance language. That doesn't mean that it's a language of love. Instead, it means that it is based on Latin, the language of the ancient Romans. French, Spanish, Portuguese, and Romanian are also Romance languages. These languages developed after the fall of the Roman

How Do You Say . . . ?

Hello	*Ciao*
Good morning	*Buongiorno*
Thank you	*Grazie*
How are you?	*Come stai?*
Good-bye	*Arrivederci*
Good	*Bene*
How much is this?	*Quanto costa questo?*
My name is . . .	*Mi chiamo . . .*

Empire. Almost every region of Italy has a dialect, or variety, of the Italian language that is named for the region, such as Lombardi, Neapolitan, and Sicilian. One section of Calabria in southern Italy incorporates a lot of Greek into its dialect because Greece colonized the region for many centuries.

Some Italian words that have entered English vocabulary include *vendetta*, *fiasco*, and *scenario*. Many Italian names of foods have also entered the English language. Examples include *pizza*, *spaghetti*, *macaroni*, *cappuccino*, and *salami*.

Speaking with Hands

Italians are known for making many hand gestures when they talk. It has been said that only half of the Italian language is in spoken words. The rest is in gestures. Some of the gestures are familiar in North America, such as the first finger held up to mean "wait a minute" or "I have something to say." An open hand held upward with the palm facing the speaker means "yeah, sure," sarcastically. Both hands, slightly cupped, with fingers together and held palms up means, "You've got to be kidding! I don't believe you!"

CHAPTER 8

A Catholic Nation

IN MOST ANCIENT RELIGIONS, INCLUDING THOSE practiced in ancient Rome and ancient Greece, people worshipped a number of gods. They thought these gods were in charge of different aspects of human life. In Greece, for example, Apollo was the god of music, the sun, and poetry. His twin sister, Artemis, was goddess of the hunt, the moon, and young girls. The king of all Greek gods was Zeus. In the religion of the ancient Romans, the gods had similar responsibilities, but most had different names. Jupiter was the king of all gods. Apollo had the same name in Greek and Roman religions, but in the Roman world, his sister was named Diana.

The Romans built many temples to their gods. Religion was important to the conduct of life. The people prayed and made offerings to the various gods.

Opposite: **A religious procession winds through the streets of Gubbio, Umbria. Many Italian towns have processions in the week leading up to Easter.**

The Pantheon

The word *pantheon* means "all gods." The Pantheon, a vast temple dedicated to all gods, was built in ancient Rome, probably about 27 BCE, and rebuilt about 125 CE. It has been in continuous use ever since. In the seventh century, it became a Roman Catholic church. It features the world's largest concrete dome that does not contain steel to make it strong.

Early Christianity

About two thousand years ago, Jesus Christ began preaching a new religion now called Christianity. Christianity reached Rome quickly, perhaps by the year 50 CE. Unlike the Roman religion, Christianity preached that there was only one god. Many Roman leaders feared that Christianity would upset the orderly Roman society, and they began to persecute Christians. Nevertheless, the religion grew.

The Roman Catholic Church holds that Peter, one of Jesus's followers, moved to Rome and there founded the Christian church. Since then, the Roman Catholic Church has been the largest sect, or version, of Christianity. Its headquarters are in Rome, in Vatican City.

The persecution of Christians stopped in 313 when Emperor Constantine issued the Edict of Milan, making it legal to be Christian in the Roman Empire. Under Constantine, Christianity became the official religion of the Roman Empire.

Peter died in about 64 CE. His successors are the popes, the leaders of the Roman Catholic Church. Most popes have been

Italian. When Karol Wojtyla of Poland was elected as Pope John Paul II in 1978, he was the first non-Italian to be chosen pope in more than 450 years. In 2013, Jorge Mario Bergoglio, an Argentine from a family of Italian immigrants, was chosen pope and became known as Pope Francis.

Pope Francis is the first pope from the Americas.

Vatican City

Located within the city of Rome is an independent nation called Vatican City. It is the headquarters of the Roman Catholic Church, built where it is said that St. Peter was buried. The smallest independent nation in the world, Vatican City extends over only 110 acres (45 hectares). Only about eight hundred people, including the pope, who is head of the Roman Catholic Church, live there. The Vatican territory was part of Rome until 1929, when Pope Pius XI and Prime Minister Benito Mussolini agreed to a treaty establishing Vatican City as a separate and independent state.

At the heart of Vatican City is St. Peter's Basilica. Construction began on the current building in 1506. Its dome is the tallest in the world, rising to 448 feet (137 m). The open square outside St. Peter's can hold eighty thousand people for special church events. Vatican City is protected by the colorfully costumed Swiss Guard, which consists of soldiers from Switzerland. The Swiss Guard has served the pope for six hundred years.

Christianity

Nearly 88 percent of the people in Italy are Roman Catholics. Far less than that, however, attend church regularly. A survey in 2005 revealed that only about 23 percent of Italian Catholics attend church at least once a month.

Catholics attend a mass in the Cathedral of Modena in northern Italy. The cathedral was built in the 1100s.

Rite of Passage

Communion is one of the most important rituals in the Roman Catholic Church. During Communion, which is central to the Catholic mass, church members eat a wafer to recall Jesus's death. Catholic children generally make their first Communion at about age seven or eight. It is an important rite of passage, the beginning of greater participation in the church. Traditionally in Italy, girls making their first Communion wear fancy white dresses and veils and often decorate their hair with flowers. Boys dress in suits for their first Communion.

A mass at a Greek Orthodox church in Venice. Greek Orthodox churches are highly decorated with icons, images of holy people.

Italy is also home to small communities of people who belong to different Catholic faiths, most notably Greek Orthodox. The Eastern churches that broke away from Roman Catholicism in 1054 follow the Orthodox faith. The Greek Orthodox Church is dominant in southern Italy, where Greek influence remained strong for many centuries.

The Reformation of the 1500s, which spread Protestantism, barely reached into Italy, probably because the Roman Catholic Church owned so much of the peninsula. Today, most Protestant churches have a small presence in Italy. The largest Protestant sect in the country is the Assemblies of God. It is a Pentecostal faith, which means the members believe in direct and personal contact with God.

Islam

Muslims, followers of the religion of Islam, first lived in Sicily and parts of mainland Italy in the ninth century. At the time, the area was under the control of Arabs, who were also Muslim. In about 1300, however, the Muslims were forced out of the country. Muslims did not return to Italy in large numbers until about 1970, when refugees from the African nation of Somalia began arriving.

In Islam, the house of worship is called a mosque. The largest mosque in Europe was built in Rome in the 1990s. Twelve thousand people can worship there. Italy is also home to about one hundred other mosques, mostly in the north.

Religion in Italy (2006 est.)	
Roman Catholic	87.8%
Other Christian	3.8%
Muslim	1.9%
Other	0.7%
Nonbeliever	5.8%

People pray at the Mosque of Rome. Muslims always pray in the direction of Mecca, Saudi Arabia, the holiest city in Islam.

Judaism

Jewish people have been living in Italy for more than two thousand years. Jews lived in ancient Rome, and there were large Jewish communities in Sicily and elsewhere in southern Italy. Over time, Jewish communities flourished in cities throughout the peninsula. They were always subject to the impulses of the Roman Catholic Church and political leaders, however. In the fifteenth century, about thirty-five thousand Jews lived in Sicily, but in 1492, they were forced to leave. Today, few Jews live on the island.

Jews pray in a synagogue in Rome. Rome has the largest Jewish population in Italy.

The nation as a whole is home to an estimated thirty thousand Jewish people. Twenty-two cities, mostly in the north, have synagogues, which are Jewish houses of worship.

Catholic nuns, women who dedicate their lives to God, do many different kinds of work. These nuns in Lombardy are creating a religious magazine.

Religious Rights

Freedom of religion is guaranteed under the constitution that created the Republic of Italy in the mid-1940s. At that time, however, the Roman Catholic Church remained the state religion. By 1984, Italy had decided to no longer have a state religion. Since then, Italians have paid a tax that is used to support organized religions. Individuals can choose which faith they want the money to go to. Currently, the Roman Catholic Church receives 87 percent of the money.

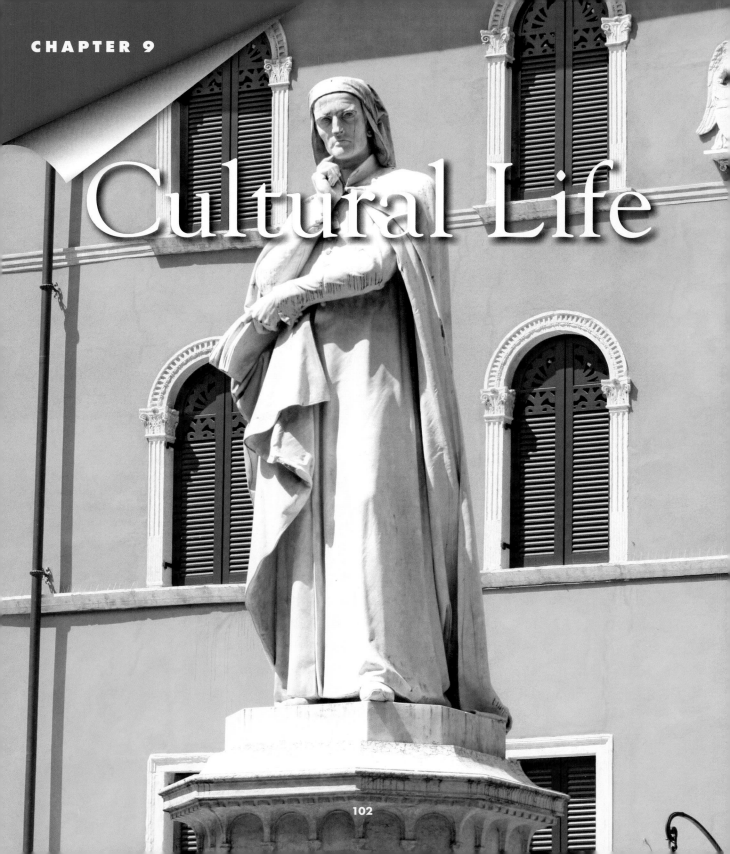

CHAPTER 9

Cultural Life

ITALIANS PRIDE THEMSELVES ON THEIR COUNTRY'S rich culture. Italian poets, novelists, painters, sculptors, composers, and filmmakers have all made major contributions to their fields. Their work, which is often groundbreaking, has stirred and influenced people around the world.

Literature

Dante Alighieri (1265–1321), usually called simply Dante, wrote one of the world's greatest works of literature. His epic poem *The Divine Comedy* describes a journey through Hell, Purgatory, and Heaven. The work is renowned for its inventive and often beautiful language.

The first Italian to win the Nobel Prize in Literature was poet Giosuè Carducci in 1906. Twenty years later, Grazia Deledda also won the Nobel Prize. Her poems and novels deal with the lives and struggles of everyday people. Playwright Luigi Pirandello won in 1934. He is best known for his play *Six*

Characters in Search of an Author, about six people who interrupt the rehearsal of a play to look for an author to finish their story. The absurd story was very influential. The Nobel Prize went to poet Salvatore Quasimodo in 1959 and poet Eugenio Montale in 1975. Playwright Dario Fo, who won in 1997, uses satire to explore important social issues.

Besides writing plays, Dario Fo also acts, directs, and runs a theater company.

Other major Italian writers include Giuseppe Tomai di Lampedusa. His 1958 novel, *The Leopard*, is about the decline of a wealthy Sicilian family during the time of unification. It was a huge international best seller. Umberto Eco, a professor at the University of Bologna, writes intricate novels that often make reference to other works of literature. His first novel, *The Name of the Rose*, is a medieval mystery that was turned into a popular film.

Umberto Eco is a novelist, philosopher, essayist, and critic.

Pinocchio

Carlo Collodi published a children's novel in 1883 called *The Adventures of Pinocchio*. It tells the story of a wooden puppet, named Pinocchio, who wants to be a real boy. Whenever Pinocchio tells a lie, his nose grows longer. This story became a classic of children's literature. Collodi also wrote novels for adults, but Pinocchio is his most lasting creation.

Michelangelo Buonarroti painted more than three hundred scenes from the Bible on the ceiling of the Sistine Chapel.

Art

Italy is home to some of the most remarkable art in the world. Some of the art, including frescoes, survived being buried in lava at Pompeii and Herculaneum. Frescoes are paintings done on wet plaster, usually on a wall or ceiling. After the plaster dries, the painting becomes a permanent part of the wall or ceiling. Many Italian frescoes still look freshly painted after two thousand years.

The Renaissance started in Italy. It was a period of great artistic and intellectual achievement. One of the greatest artists of the time was Michelangelo Buonarroti (1475–1564), who was renowned for both painting and sculpture. His detailed painting covering the ceiling of the Sistine Chapel at the Vatican is one of the great artworks of the world. He spent

Renaissance Man

Leonardo da Vinci (1452–1519), who was born in Florence, is considered a Renaissance man. This means that he did great things in many fields, including art, architecture, science, and mechanics. He was curious about everything. Leonardo's painting titled *Mona Lisa* is one of the world's most famous portraits. His

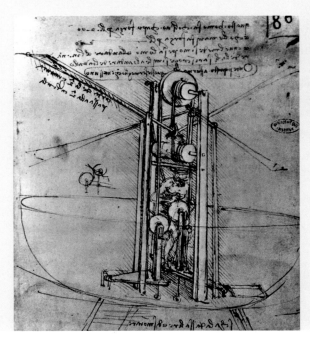

sketch called *Vitruvian Man* appears on the Italian €1 coin and is one of the world's most reproduced pieces of art, appearing on T-shirts, greeting cards, posters, and much more. His painting *The Last Supper*, which is on the wall of a church in Milan, is one of the most reproduced religious paintings. Leonardo was also an engineer and inventor. He filled journals with sketches of his ideas, which included everything from solar power to musical instruments to flying machines (left).

most of four years, from 1508 to 1512, standing on high scaffolding, craning his neck while painting the ceiling. His *Pietà*, a sculpture of Mary, the mother of Jesus, holding Jesus after he died, is also in the Vatican.

Many other great Italian artists also created pieces for the Vatican and churches throughout Italy. They include Titian, Raphael, Gian Lorenzo Bernini, Sandro Botticelli, Fra Angelico, Giotto, and Lorenzo Ghiberti.

Lorenzo Ghiberti created magnificent bronze images for the doors of the Baptistery of Florence Cathedral.

Italian artists have also flourished in more recent times. In the early twentieth century, Amedeo Modigliani painted strong, modern portraits in which the people appear elongated. Giorgio de Chirico painted mysterious landscapes filled with large objects that wouldn't be found in such settings. His paintings, which did not show the realistic world, had a strong influence on later painters called surrealists.

Opera

Music has also flourished in Italy. The piano, a basic instrument in much music today, was invented in Italy. In about 1709, Bartolomeo Cristofori, working in Florence, converted the much older harpsichord into an instrument that was easier to play. It was originally called the pianoforte, meaning "soft-loud," because the volume could change. The loudness of the harpsichord could not be varied.

Opera consists of dramatic stories told in song. Parts that would be spoken in a regular play are sung. Opera began in Italy in the early 1600s, mainly with the work of Claudio Monteverdi (1567–1643). Since then, opera has been part of the Italian culture. Other major opera composers include Giuseppe Verdi, Giacomo Puccini, and Gaetano Donizetti. Many opera composers also wrote oratorios. These are religious works sung by large choruses and soloists. Antonio Vivaldi (1678–1741) was one of the first to write such pieces.

Many of the finest opera singers in the world have come from Italy. At the turn of the twentieth century, tenor Enrico Caruso introduced much of the world to opera. Luciano

The figures in the paintings of Amedeo Modigliani typically have very long necks.

Luciano Pavarotti was renowned for his pure tone. He was greatly popular even beyond opera lovers.

Pavarotti, who died in 2007, was one of the greatest tenors of recent times, and Andrea Bocelli is a popular tenor who performs internationally. In 2009, three teenagers with fine operatic voices formed a pop-opera group called Il Volo, "the flight." They have become popular in the United States.

Today's Music

It used to be that Italian children grew up knowing and singing Italian opera, but that is no longer the case. Rap, punk, rock, and other popular music forms have taken root in Italy. Tiziano Ferro creates modern versions of rhythm and blues music. Gianna Nannini has been popular since the 1970s when she had her first hit "America," from the album *California*.

Popular rock artists include Vasco Rossi and Luciano Ligabue. A top band since about 2005 is Negramaro. Some of their music is heard in the *Guitar Hero* music video games.

The Sanremo Festival is a song contest held in February in the town of San Remo on the Italian Riviera. The contest, first held in 1951, has launched the careers of many Italian singers. Pop singer Gianni Morandi won the Sanremo Festival in 1987. Since then, he has been awarded many gold records and has hosted the festival.

The success of the San Remo contest inspired the creation of the Eurovision Song Contest, which first took place in 1954. The contest features competitors from around Europe. Italian singers won it in 1964 and 1990. The event is always shown on TV, making it one of the longest running broadcasts in the world.

Movie Time

Italian films blossomed in the years after World War II. Many of those produced immediately following the war were in a style called neorealism. These films, such as *The Bicycle Thief* and *Rome, Open City*, showed the difficult life people faced in their devastated country. Leading neorealist filmmakers were Roberto Rossellini, Luchino Visconti, and Vittorio De Sica. Other major filmmakers include Federico Fellini and Franco Zeffirelli. Lina Wertmüller, an Italian of Swiss heritage, was the first female director to be nominated for an Oscar, for her 1975 film *Seven Beauties*.

Marcello Mastroianni was a leading man for decades. Anna Magnani won an Oscar for Best Actress for her perfor-

The Bicycle Thief, directed by Vittorio De Sica, tells the story of a father and son searching for their stolen bicycle, which the father desperately needs for his job. It is generally considered one of the greatest films of all time.

mance as a Sicilian widow in the 1955 movie *The Rose Tattoo*.

In the 1960s, many films were made in Italy that imitated American westerns. They were called spaghetti westerns. Some of the best-known spaghetti westerns, such as *A Fistful of Dollars*, were directed by Sergio Leone and starred American actor Clint Eastwood. Many of these movies were filmed in Sardinia.

Racing Sports

Cycling is very popular throughout Italy. Until World War II, it was the nation's most popular sport. A bicycle race called Giro d'Italia has been held annually since 1909. This twenty-three-day race takes riders through the Alps before ending in Milan.

Formula One car racing is hugely popular in Italy. Formula One cars are single-seat, high-performance cars with uncovered wheels. The Italian Grand Prix has been raced at Monza, north of Milan, since 1922. Drivers race around the track at more than 200 miles per hour (320 kph).

Anna Magnani was one of Italy's greatest actors. She was known for performances that conveyed deep, genuine emotion.

Racing Around the Square

Twice each year, ten horseback riders race around the huge town square in the center of the Tuscan town of Siena. The event is called the Palio. Each rider, dressed in a medieval costume and riding bareback, represents a different neighborhood of Siena. Thousands of spectators jam the square to watch the race, which generally lasts only about ninety seconds. The Palio, which also includes a colorful pageant, dates back to the 1600s.

Big-Time Sports

Soccer, known as football outside of North America, is the most popular sport in Italy. The most important soccer tournament in the world is the World Cup. It is held every four years, and Italy has won it four times, in 1934, 1938, 1982, and 2006. Only Brazil has won more often.

Major cities in Italy have at least one team. The most successful team through the years has been Juventus, in Turin. Most big teams, as well as most towns, support programs for young people to learn to play the game. Many local soccer teams involve just about anyone who wants to play.

Olympic Games

Italy has hosted the Olympics three times. In 1956, the Winter Games were held at Cortina d'Ampezzo in the Dolomite Mountains of northern Italy. Four years later, the Summer Games were held in Rome. Then, in 2006, Italy hosted the Winter Games in and around Turin.

One of the most famous Italian athletes is skier Alberto Tomba. He won five Olympic gold medals in the 1988 Winter Games. Italians took twenty-eight medals, eight of them gold, in the 2012 London Olympics. Fencer Valentina Vezzali won her seventh and eighth medals in those games, making her one of Italy's most decorated athletes.

Fencer Valentina Vezzali celebrates a victory at the 2012 Olympics.

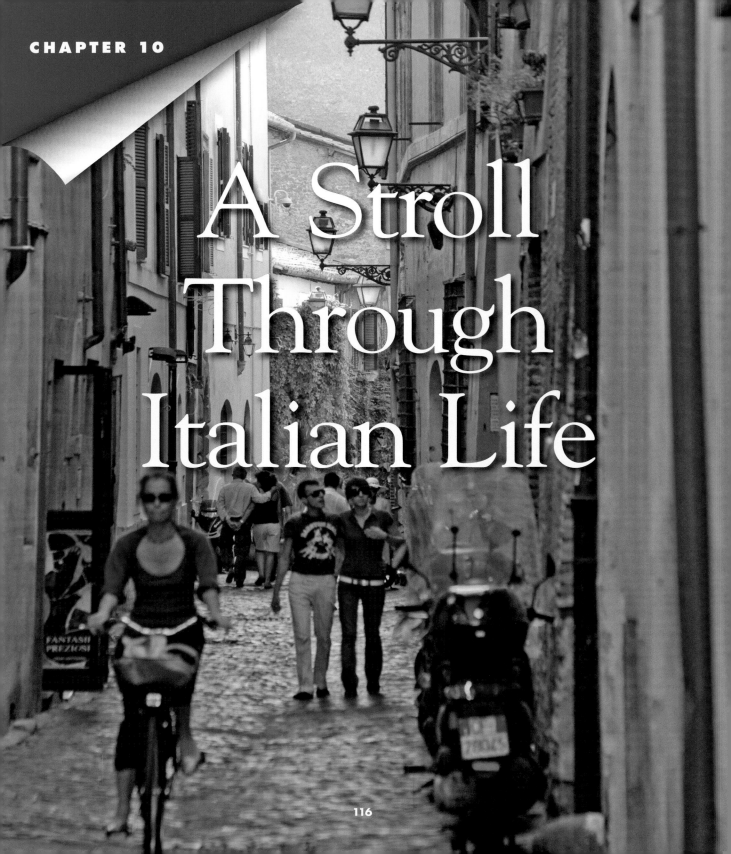

CHAPTER 10

A Stroll Through Italian Life

AS THE DAY WINDS DOWN, MANY ITALIANS TAKE a stroll, chatting and greeting friends and neighbors. On Sunday, this time is called *la passeggiata.* During evenings when the weather is nice, many people dress up and walk through their neighborhood. They may pick up a few items at a fruit stand or stop for a coffee, talking all the while.

Opposite: **Italians and visitors alike enjoy walking through Rome's narrow backstreets.**

City and Country

Two-thirds of Italians live north of Rome, and one-third live south of it. The north tends to be wealthier and more industrial. Italian cities are crowded, and most people live in apartments. Some wealthy people have vacation houses on lakes or at the seaside. In rural areas, especially in the south, farmers and their families usually live in villages or towns. They drive or bicycle to their farmland each day.

The Neighborhood Barista

Italian neighborhoods usually feature bars. A bar is a place to stop for a coffee, a quick sandwich, a *gelato* (ice cream), or just a look at a newspaper. A bar usually charges customers more to sit at a table (perhaps outside in the sunshine) than to stand at the bar. The person who makes and serves the coffee is called a *barista*.

Going to School

All children in Italy must go to school between the ages of six and sixteen. School is divided into kindergarten, primary school, lower secondary (middle school), upper secondary (high school), and university. Students in secondary school may prepare to go to university or to receive technical training. Different high schools may focus on different subjects, such as languages, arts, classics, or science. Public school is free.

The school year lasts from September through June. For most students, school ends early in the day, around 1:00 p.m., but they also go to school on Saturdays. Traditionally, the big meal of the day was after the children arrived home from school. Shops closed, and parents came home from work for the family to eat together. This pattern is gradually disappearing, and many stores now stay open through the noon hour. Some city schools have increased the length of the day during the week and no longer hold Saturday classes.

In 2012, 98.4 percent of Italians could read and write. However, only 54 percent of adults between the ages of twenty-five and sixty-four had earned high school diplomas. Adults in the north of Italy are more likely to have completed high school than those in the south.

Italy is the site of dozens of universities, including many of the world's oldest universities. The University of Bologna was founded in 1088. Many people consider it the oldest university in the world. Dante went to school there seven hundred years ago. Maria Gaetana Agnesi (1718–1799), who was the first-known woman to write a mathematics book, taught at the University of Bologna. She is believed to be the first woman to teach mathematics at a university. Today, more than eighty thousand students attend the University of Bologna. Its law school is especially highly regarded.

From Philosophy to Physics

As a high school student in Milan, Fabiola Gianotti was more interested in literature and philosophy than science. Gradually, she came to believe that physics could answer many of the questions about the fundamental nature of the world. She went on to earn a PhD in physics from the University of Milan. Today, Gianotti leads an important group of physicists at CERN, the European Organization for Nuclear Research. For years, scientists at CERN hunted for Higgs boson, a basic particle that forms all the other particles that make up atoms. Scientists had first proposed the existence of Higgs boson in 1964. In 2012, Gianotti announced that physicists at CERN had finally confirmed its existence.

Sweet Treat

Gelato is Italian ice cream. It is typically denser and more intensely flavored than most American ice cream. Gelato may have first been made in the Roman Empire, when wealthy people would have snow and ice brought down from the mountains to be made into this treat. Today, most gelato shops and carts in Italy still feature homemade gelato.

Pizza and Pasta

Mention Italy and many people will think of pizza and pasta. Pizza probably originated as a flatbread on which people put different toppings. It was first given the name *pizza* in Gaeta, north of Naples, in the year 977. Tomatoes were not part of the toppings until about the seventeenth century, because they are native to the Western Hemisphere. Until explorers and traders were traveling back and forth from

Mediterranean Diet

People in southern Italy traditionally ate what is called the Mediterranean diet. This is a diet rich in vegetables, beans, and olive oil. The Mediterranean diet features only moderate amounts of dairy products and little red meat. Scientists have discovered that this tends to be a very healthy way of eating. People who follow this diet are much less likely to have heart disease than people who eat more meat and dairy products. The common diet in southern Italy is changing, however. People there are now eating more like the average American, with greater quantities of meat, junk food, and quick snacks.

Europe to the Americas, there were no tomatoes in Europe. Italians began adding cheese to their pizza in the nineteenth century. Today, Italians put anything on a pizza, including potatoes, eggs, and peas.

Pasta is a staple food of many countries, but it is most associated with Italy. The country is known for its great variety of pasta shapes. Some are long and thin, like vermicelli, spaghetti, and linguini. Others, like penne and rigatoni, are tube-shaped. Still others, like fusilli, are spirals. It is estimated that Italians eat 60 pounds (27 kg) of pasta each year. They often serve a small dish of it as an appetizer before the main course at dinner. Pasta can be served many ways, such as with a red sauce or a creamy white sauce or with vegetables. In Italy it is often served with just a little tasty olive oil on it. Pasta can also be filled with different ingredients, making such dishes as ravioli or tortellini.

In Italy, pizza is often cooked in a wood-burning oven.

Truffles

Truffles are mushrooms that grow underground. They are a specialty in Tuscany and Piedmont. Truffle hunters use dogs with a powerful sense of smell to sniff out these mushrooms. Italy's white truffles are incredibly valuable. In 2007, a truffle weighing 3.3 pounds (1.5 kg) sold for US$330,000. Some towns in the north, such as Alba and San Miniato, have special festivals celebrating truffle season in the autumn.

Wine and Cheese

Italy produces more wine than any other country. It produced about 18 percent of the world's supply in 2010. Winemaking was introduced into Italy by the Greeks no later than 800 BCE. Today, vineyards cover sunny hillsides from the Alps down to the southern tip of Italy and on to the islands. The first Italian wine to become popular in the United States was Chianti, a red wine that came in a bottle nestled in a straw basket. The most popular Italian white wine in the United States now is pinot grigio.

Hundreds of different kinds of cheeses are made in Italy.

Several of the world's most popular cheeses originated in Italy. Parmesan, which frequently is sprinkled on pasta dishes, originated in Parma, a city in northern Italy. Mozzarella, a standard part of pizza today, originated in the southernmost part of Italy, where it was first made from the milk of water buffalo. It is also often made from cow's

Let's Make Caprese

Some of the best Italian recipes are the simplest. Have an adult help you make this simple mozzarella, tomato, and basil salad called caprese.

Ingredients

4 large tomatoes

1 pound fresh mozzarella cheese

8 to10 leaves fresh basil

4 tablespoons extra virgin olive oil

Salt and pepper

Directions

Slice the tomatoes and mozzarella cheese to the same thickness. Put one slice of mozzarella at the edge of a plate. Place one basil leaf overlapping the mozzarella, and then one slice tomato overlapping the basil. Start again with the mozzarella, alternating ingredients until they make a complete circle around the plate. Drizzle olive oil over the salad and sprinkle with salt and pepper. Enjoy!

Public Holidays

New Year's Day	January 1
Epiphany	January 6
Unification Day	March 17
Easter Monday	March or April
Liberation Day	April 25
Labor Day	May 1
Republic Day	June 2
Assumption Day	August 15
All Saints' Day	November 1
Immaculate Conception	December 8
Christmas Day	December 25
St. Stephen's Day	December 26

milk. Fontina cheese is made in the Aosta Valley. It can be mild or strong in flavor, depending on how it's made. Italians are still coming up with new types of cheeses. A man working near

Italian police officers take part in a parade on Republic Day.

Milan invented Bel Paese in the early twentieth century. It is a soft, buttery cheese that can be used like mozzarella.

Holidays and Celebrations

The Italian constitution guarantees Italian workers at least four weeks of vacation every year. Most Italians take the month of August off as a long vacation. Sometimes stores are closed for the entire month. Italians who can afford it go to the mountains or ocean beaches to cool off. Some families have been going to the same beach for several generations, ever since ocean swimming became popular.

A boy jumps over a boardwalk between rows of beach shelters in Tuscany. Many Italian beaches rent shelters to vacationers.

A Stroll Through Italian Life   **125**

On June 24 each year, a brutal soccer game called *calcio fiorentino* is played in Florence. Players can use both their hands and their feet.

Historic festivals often involve sports. One of the biggest days of the year in Florence is June 24, a day that honors the city's patron saint, John the Baptist. Florence has held a soccer match on June 24 every year since 1688. This is not the usual type of soccer game, but a brutal match played by twenty-seven-member teams in costume. They play an old-fashioned version of the game that allows punching, elbowing, and other violent tactics.

Many Italian towns have great festivals known as Carnival just before Lent, the somber period leading up to Easter. In villages, Carnival is typically just a small gathering. But Carnival in the city of Venice features a huge parade of masked revelers.

This tradition dates back to at least the 1400s. People stroll through the streets wearing ornate masks and Renaissance outfits. It is a perfect way to end a tour of Italy, recalling the nation's proud past while living life to the fullest in the present.

In Venice, Carnival participants dress in elaborate costumes with often somber masks.

Gifts from La Befana

Christmas celebrations continue into January in Italy. Epiphany is a holiday that falls on January 6, twelve days after Christmas. Tradition says that this is the day when the Three Wise Men arrived with gifts at the manger where Jesus was born. In Italy, children hang their stockings up before going to bed on January 5. In the morning, they will find gifts and candy in their stockings if they've been good, or they might find coal if they haven't been good. It is said that these gifts are left by La Befana, a good witch. "Befana" probably comes from the word *epiphany*. On January 6, men dressed as La Befana race boats on the Grand Canal of Venice.

Timeline

ITALIAN HISTORY		WORLD HISTORY	
		ca. 2500 BCE	The Egyptians build the pyramids and the Sphinx in Giza.
Greeks begin building colonies in Italy.	ca. 800 BCE		
Etruscans develop a powerful civilization.	700s BCE	ca. 563 BCE	The Buddha is born in India.
The Roman Republic is established.	ca. 509 BCE		
Julius Caesar gains control of Rome.	49 BCE		
Julius Caesar is assassinated; the Roman Republic ends.	44 BCE		
Augustus Caesar becomes the first Roman emperor.	27 BCE		
Mt. Vesuvius erupts, burying Pompeii and Herculaneum.	79 CE		
Emperor Diocletian splits the Roman Empire into two parts.	293		
		313 CE	The Roman emperor Constantine legalizes Christianity.
The Roman Empire falls.	476		
The Lombards control much of Italy.	564–774	610	The Prophet Muhammad begins preaching a new religion called Islam.
		1054	The Eastern (Orthodox) and Western (Roman Catholic) Churches break apart.
		1095	The Crusades begin.
		1215	King John seals the Magna Carta.
The Renaissance begins in Italy.	1300s	1300s	The Renaissance begins in Italy.
		1347	The plague sweeps through Europe.
		1453	Ottoman Turks capture Constantinople, conquering the Byzantine Empire.
		1492	Columbus arrives in North America.

ITALIAN HISTORY

Spain, Austria, and France vie for control of Italy.	**1500s– early 1800s**
The Kingdom of Italy is established.	**1861**
Italy enters World War I on the side of the Allies.	**1915**
Benito Mussolini becomes prime minister of Italy.	**1922**
Italy conquers Ethiopia.	**1936**
Mussolini forms an alliance with Nazi Germany.	**1939**
Italy surrenders to the Allies during World War II.	**1943**
Italians vote to replace their monarchy with a republic.	**1946**
Italy is a founding member of the European Economic Community.	**1957**
The terrorist group the Red Brigades kidnaps and kills Prime Minister Aldo Moro.	**1978**
Many politicians are arrested in an anticorruption program.	**Early 1990s**
Italy begins to use the euro as its currency.	**2002**
An earthquake hits Abruzzo, killing hundreds of people.	**2009**

WORLD HISTORY

1500s	Reformers break away from the Catholic Church, and Protestantism is born.
1776	The U.S. Declaration of Independence is signed.
1789	The French Revolution begins.
1865	The American Civil War ends.
1879	The first practical lightbulb is invented.
1914	World War I begins.
1917	The Bolshevik Revolution brings communism to Russia.
1929	A worldwide economic depression begins.
1939	World War II begins.
1945	World War II ends.
1969	Humans land on the Moon.
1975	The Vietnam War ends.
1989	The Berlin Wall is torn down as communism crumbles in Eastern Europe.
1991	The Soviet Union breaks into separate states.
2001	Terrorists attack the World Trade Center in New York City and the Pentagon near Washington, D.C.
2004	A tsunami in the Indian Ocean destroys coastlines in Africa, India, and Southeast Asia.
2008	The United States elects its first African American president.

Fast Facts

Official name: Republic of Italy

Capital: Rome

Official language: Italian

Rome

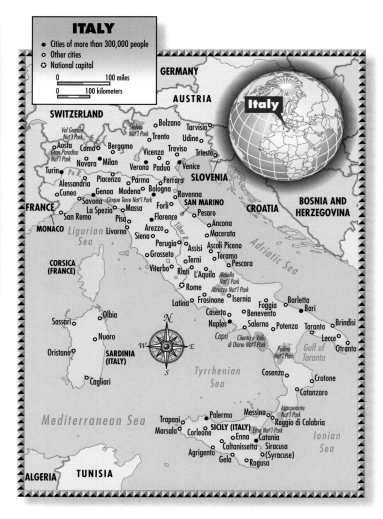

Italian flag

Dolomites

Official religion:	None
Year of founding:	1861, Kingdom of Italy; 1946, Republic of Italy
National anthem:	"Fratelli d'Italia" ("Brothers of Italy")
Form of government:	Republic
Head of state:	President
Head of government:	Prime minister
Area of country:	116,320 square miles (301,267 sq km)
Bordering countries:	France to the northwest, Switzerland and Austria to the north, Slovenia to the northeast
Highest elevation:	Mont Blanc, 15,781 feet (4,810 m) above sea level
Lowest elevation:	Near Ferrara, 13 feet (4 m) below sea level
Average high temperature:	In Milan, 40°F (5°C) in January and 84°F (29°C) in July; in Palermo, 59°F (15°C) in January and 83°F (28°C) in July
Average annual precipitation:	32 inches (81 cm) in Rome

Naples

Currency

National population (2012 est.):	61,261,254	
Population of major cities (2012 est.):	Rome	3,357,000
	Milan	2,962,000
	Naples	2,270,000
	Turin	1,662,000
	Palermo	872,000

Population density: 513 per square mile (198 per sq km)

Landmarks:
- ▶ *Colosseum*, Rome
- ▶ *Leaning Tower*, Pisa
- ▶ *Milan Cathedral*, Milan
- ▶ *Pompeii*, near Naples
- ▶ *Sistine Chapel*, Vatican City

Economy: Tourism is Italy's largest industry. Service industries such as trade, restaurants, hotels, banking, and real estate provide 73 percent of Italy's national income, and manufacturing industries provide about 25 percent. Italy's most valuable mineral product is natural gas. Marble and granite are important quarried products. Rock salt, feldspar, and potash are also mined.

Currency: The euro. In 2013, US$1.32 equaled €1, and €0.76 equaled US$1.

System of weights and measures: Metric system

Literacy rate (2012): 98.4%

Teenagers

Anna Magnani

Common Italian words and phrases:

Ciao	Hello
Grazie	Thank you
Come stai?	How are you?
Arrivederci	Good-bye
Quanto costa questo?	How much is this?
Mi chiamo . . .	My name is . . .

Prominent Italians:

Dante Alighieri (1265–1321)
Poet

Michelangelo Buonarroti (1475–1564)
Painter, sculptor, architect

Galileo Galilei (1564–1642)
Scientist

Giuseppe Garibaldi (1807–1882)
General

Anna Magnani (1908–1973)
Actor

Marco Polo (1254–1324)
Traveler and writer

Miuccia Prada (1949–)
Clothing designer

Roberto Rossellini (1906–1977)
Film director

Giuseppe Verdi (1813–1901)
Composer

Leonardo da Vinci (1452–1519)
Painter, sculptor, scientist

To Find Out More

Books

► Dyan, Penelope, and John R. Weigand. *When in Rome: A Kid's Guide to Rome*. Jamul, CA: Bellissima Publishing, 2009.

► Lace, William W. *The Vatican*. San Diego: Lucent Books, 2004.

► James, Simon. *Ancient Rome*. New York: DK Children, 2008.

► Wilkinson, Philip. *Michelangelo: The Young Artist Who Dreamed of Perfection*. Washington, DC: National Geographic, 2006.

Music

► Il Volo, *Il Volo*. Santa Monica, CA: Geffen, 2011.

► Luciano Pavarotti. *Pavarotti's Greatest Hits*. London: Decca, 2007.

► *Putumayo Presents: Italia*. New York: Putumayo, 2009.

> ▶ Visit this Scholastic Web site for more information on Italy:
> www.factsfornow.scholastic.com
> Enter the keyword Italy

Index

Page numbers in *italics*
indicate illustrations.

A

Abruzzo National Park, 29
Abruzzo region, 24
Adriatic Sea, 15, 18, 22, 72, 82
Aeolian Islands, 24
agriculture
    cropland, 71
    crops, 20, *20*, *70*, 71–72
    economy and, 56, 73
    immigrants and, 87
    Latium Plain, 20, *20*
    livestock, 31, 34
    olives, 32–33, *33*, 72
    Po Valley, 71
    prehistoric cultures, 39
    Puglia region, 21
    rice, 72
    vineyards, 20, *20*, 31, 122
    wheat, 71–72
air pollution, 36, 37
Alboin, king of the Lombards, *44*
Allied Powers, 54, *55*
Alps mountain range, 15
animal life
    alpine ibexes, 30, 33
    Apennine brown bears, 29–30
    bearded vultures, 33
    birds, 31–32, *32*, 33, 35
    Bonelli's eagles, 35
    cirl buntings, 32, *32*

    Colosseum and, 79
    deer, 31
    hoopoes, 32
    hunting, 32, 39
    Italian wolves, 31, *31*, 35
    livestock, 31, 34
    mouflons (wild sheep), 30, *30*
    songbirds, 32, *32*
    Umbri culture and, 39
    waterbirds, 31
    wild boars, 31
Antony, Mark, 43
Apennine Mountains, 15, 19–20, *19*,
    25, 31
archaeology, 79
architecture, 18, 48, 49, 62, 83, 107
art
    Amedeo Modigliani, 108, *109*
    art-glassmaking industry, 81
    Baptistery of Florence Cathedral,
        108
    currency and, 83
    Etruscan culture, *38*
    frescoes, 106–107, *106*
    Giorgio de Chirico, 108
    Herculaneum, 106
    Leonardo da Vinci, 48–49, 107,
        107, 133
    Medici family and, 48–49, *48*
    Michelangelo Buonarroti, 48, *48*,
        106–107, *106*, 133
    Pompeii, 106
    Renaissance, 47–49, 106
    Rome and, 62
    sculpture, *38*, *48*, 106, 107
    tourism and, 80
autonomous regions, 69
Autostrada, 74
Axis Powers, 54

B

banking industry, 19, 73, 78

Baptistery of Florence Cathedral, *108*
Berlusconi, Silvio, *58*, 59, 65
birds, 31–32, *32*, 33, 35
Bologna, 37, *37*, 74
borders, 15, 17
Byzantine Catholic Church, 44

C

Caesar, Augustus, 42
Caesar, Julius, 42, 43
Cagliari, 22
Calabria region, 51, 91
capital city. *See* Rome.
Capitoline Hill, 62
Carabinieri (police force), 68
Carnival, 126–127, *127*
Carrara, *81*, 82
Carthaginian culture, 41–42
Castel Nuovo (New Castle), 27
Catholicism. *See* Greek Orthodox
    Church; Roman Catholic Church.
CERN (European Organization for
    Nuclear Research), 119
Chamber of Deputies, *60*, 63, *63*
Charlemagne, Holy Roman emperor,
    44
Charles V, Holy Roman emperor, 49
children, *11*, 88–89, 97, *97*, *125*
Christian Democratic Party, 55
Cinque Terre National Park, 34–35, *34*
cities. *See also* Milan; Rome; towns;
    villages.
    Bologna, 37, *37*, 74
    Cagliari, 22
    Cortona, *13*
    Florence, 47, 48, 49, 109, 126, *126*
    Gaeta, 120
    Genoa, 18, 73
    Herculaneum, 24, *24*, 106
    L'Aquila, 24
    Messina, 25
    Monza, 113

Naples, 27, *27*, 46, 50, 51, *84*, 87
Paestum, *40*
Palermo, 21, *51*, 87
Pavia, 18, *44*
Pompeii, 24, 106
Taranto, 36
Treviso, 77
Turin, 27, 73, 74, 87, 114
Venice, 18, 36, *36*, 45, *46*, 81, 98, 126, 127, *127*
Verona, *102*
city-states, 45, *45*, 49
Cleopatra, queen of Egypt, 43, *43*
climate, 21, 25–26, *25*, 35, 36
clothing, 12, 126, *126*, 127, *127*
coal, 82
coalitions, 61, 64
coastline, 15, 17, *17*, 21, 26, 32
colonies, 52, *52*
Colosseum, 8, 79, *79*, 83
communications, 58, 59, 74, *101*
communism, 53, 57
Congress of Vienna, 50
Constantine, emperor of Rome, 43, 94
constitution, 66, *66*, 101, 125
Constitutional Court, 66, *66*
Cosa Nostra, 58
Count of Cavour, 52
Courts of Assizes, 66
Cristofori, Bartolomeo, 109
crops, 20, *20*, *70*, 71–72
currency (euro), 58, 83, *83*

D

Dante Alighieri, 13, 47–48, *102*, 103, 119, 133
De Gasperi, Alcide, 55
Deledda, Grazia, 103
dictatorships, 53
Diocletian, emperor of Rome, 43
Dolomite Mountains, *14*, 30
Ducati company, 74–75

E

earthquakes, 22, 23, *24*, 25
Eastern Roman Empire, 43
economy
    agriculture, 56, 73
    banking industry, 19, 73, 78
    communism and, 53
    currency (euro), 58, 83, *83*
    European Union (EU), 58
    imports, 76
    industrial triangle, 73
    jobs, 36, 58, 71, 76, 78, 87, 89
    manufacturing, 56, *56*, 73, 74–77, *75*
    Mario Monti and, 65
    mining, 73, 81–82, *81*
    San Marino, 19
    service industries, 78, *78*, 80
    steelmaking industry, 75–76, *75*
    stock exchange, 73
    taxes, 58, 69, 89, 101
    textile industry, 76–77, *77*
    tourism, 19, 78, *80*
    trade, 18, 40, 58
Edict of Milan, 94
education, 9–10, 59, *78*, 118–119
Elba, 22
elections, 41, 55, 61, 63, 64, 65, 68, 69
elevation, *14*, 15, 17
emigration, 88, *88*
Emilia-Romagna region, 19, 45
energy, 82–83, *82*
environmental protection, 36–37
Erice, *26*
Eritrea, 52
Ethiopia, 52
ethnic groups, 85–87, *86*
Etna National Park, 35
Etruscan culture, *38*, 40, 41
euro (currency), 58, 83, *83*
European Economic Community (EEC), 56, 58
European Space Agency, 77

European Union (EU), 58, 59, 71
evergreen trees, 32
executive branch of government, 52, 53, 55, *58*, 59, 62, 63, *63*, 64–65, 68, 69, 96
exploration, 47

F

families, 10, 88–89, *89*, 118
Fascist Party, 53, *53*, 54
fashion industry, 27, 133
fencing, 115, *115*
festivals, 126
Fiat company, 56, 74
fishing industry, 72–73
flag, 68, *68*
Florence, 47, 48, 49, 109, 126, *126*
Fo, Dario, 104, *104*
foods, 9, 10, 11, 32–33, 71, 78, 90, 91, 118, 120–121, *120*, *121*, 122, *122*, 123, *123*
Formula One car racing, 113
Francis (pope), 95, *95*
Frankish tribes, 44
frescoes, 106–107, *106*

G

Galileo Galilei, 49, *49*, 133
Garibaldi, Giuseppe, 50–51, *50*, *51*, 133
gelato (ice cream), 11, 120, *120*
Genoa, 18, 73
geography
    borders, 15, 17
    coastline, 15, 17, *17*, 21, 26, 32
    earthquakes, 22, 23, *24*, 25
    elevation, *14*, 15, 17
    glaciers, 16, 20
    lakes, 17, 34
    land area, 17
    mountains, *14*, 15–16, *16*, 17, 19, *19*, 21, 25

rivers, 17, 18, 20, *20*
tectonic plates, 23
volcanoes, 17, 21, 23–24, *23*, 35
Germanic tribes, 43, 44
Germany, 52, 54, 55, 75, 76
Gianotti, Fabiola, 119, *119*
glaciers, 16, 20
gladiators, 79, *79*
glassmaking industry, 81
government
    Chamber of Deputies, 60, 63, *63*
    coalitions, 61, 64
    constitution, 66, *66*, 101, 125
    Constitutional Court, 66, *66*
    corruption in, 57, 58
    Courts of Assizes, 66
    dictatorships, 53
    elections, 41, 55, 61, 63, 64, 65,
        68, 69
    environmental protection, 37
    executive branch, 52, 53, 55, 58,
        59, 62, 63, *63*, 64–65, 68, 69,
        96
    independence, 49, 50, *50*, 64
    judicial branch, 65, 66, *66*, 68
    laws, 76
    legislative branch, 52, 60, 61, 62,
        63–64, *63*, 65, 68, 69
    military, 68, 96, *96*
    monarchs, 51–52
    Parliament, 61, 63–64, *63*, 68
    police forces, 68
    political parties, 53, 55, 61, 64
    presidents, 62, 63, 64, 65, 68, 69
    prime ministers, 52, 53, 55, 58, 59,
        63, 64–65, 96
    regional governments, 68–69
    religion and, 101
    Roman Empire, 41
    Senate, 64
    Supreme Court of Cassation, 66
    taxes, 58, 69, 89, 101

Grand Canal, 127, *127*
Gran Paradiso National Park, 30, 33
Greek culture, 40, *40*
Greek Orthodox Church, 98, *98*
Gulf of Venice, 18
Gypsies. *See* Romani people.

H
Hannibal (Carthaginian general), 42
Herculaneum, 24, *24*, 106
Higgs boson, 119
historical maps. *See also* maps.
    Italian City-States, 1500, *45*
    Italian Colonies in Africa, 1937, *52*
    People of Italy, 500 BCE, *40*
    Roman Empire, *42*
Hitler, Adolf, 54
holidays
    national, 52, 124, *124*
    religious, *92*, 127, *127*
housing, 39, 87, 89, 117
hunting, 32, 39
hydroelectricity, 83
hypogeum, 79

I
immigrants, 87, 89
imports, 76
independence, 49, 50, *50*, 64
industrial triangle, 73
International Space Station, 77
Islamic religion, 99, *99*
islands
    Aeolian Islands, 24
    Elba, 22
    Murano, 81
    Sardinia, 21, 22, *22*, 33, 45, 50, 51,
        64, 69, 112
    Sicily, 17, 21, 23, *23*, 25, 26, 35, 46,
        50, 51, 54, *55*, 58, 68, 69, 99, 100
    Tremiti Islands, 22
    Tuscan Archipelago, 22

Venice, 18, 36, *36*, 45, 46, 81, 98,
    126, 127, *127*
Italian language, 48
Italian Riviera, 18, 111
Italian Social Republic, 55
Italian wolves (national animal), 31,
    31, 35

J
jobs, 36, 58, 71, 76, 78, 87, 89
John Paul II (pope), 95
Judaism, 100–101, *100*
judicial branch of government, 65, 66,
    66, 68
Juventus soccer team, 114

K
Khan, Kublai, 47
Kingdom of Lombardy, 44, *44*, 45
Kingdom of Naples, 46, 50
Kingdom of Sardinia, 45–46
Kingdom of Sicily, 46, 50

L
languages, 12–13, 16, 47–48, 90–91, *90*
L'Aquila, 24
Latin language, 47
Latium Plain, 20, *20*
Lazio region, *19*, 45
Leaning Tower of Pisa, 18, *18*
legislative branch of government, 52,
    60, 61, 62, 63–64, *63*, 65, 68, 69
Leonardo da Vinci, 48–49, 107, *107*,
    133
Leone, Sergio, 112
Letta, Enrico, 65
Libya, 52
Ligabue, Luciano, 111
Ligurian Sea, 29, 72
literacy rate, 118
literature, 47–48, *102*, 103–105, *104*,
    105, 133

livestock, 31, 34
Lombard tribe, 44, *44*
Lombardy region, 44, *44*, 45, 68, 72, *101*

M

Machiavelli, Niccolò, 49
Mafia, 57, 58
Magnani, Anna, 111–112, *113*, 133, *133*
manufacturing, 56, *56*, 73, 74–77, *75*
maps. *See also* historical maps.
    geopolitical, *10*
    population density, 88
    regions, 69
    resources, *72*
    Rome, *62*
    topographical, *17*
marble, 81–82, *81*
Marche region, 19, 45
marine life, 29, 31, 72–73
Medici family, 48–49, *48*, 64
Mediterranean diet, 120, *120*
Mediterranean Sea, 15, 29, 52, 82
Messina, 25
Michelangelo Buonarroti, 48, *48*, 106–107, *106*, 133
Middle Ages, 45–47, *46*
Milan
    art, 107
    banking industry, 73
    climate, *25*
    fashion industry, 27, 76–77
    flag of, 68
    Giro d'Italia bicycle race, 113
    immigrants in, 86
    industrial triangle and, 73
    Lambretta manufacturing, 75
    Milan Cathedral, 27, *27*
    population, 27, 87
military, 68, 96, *96*
mining, 73, 81–82, *81*
monarchs, 51–52

Montale, Eugenio, 104
Mont Blanc, 15–16, *16*, 17
Monteverdi, Claudio, 109
mosques, 99, *99*
Mount Etna, 17, 21, 23, *23*, 35
Mount Vesuvius, 23–24
movies, 111–112, *112*, *113*, 133, *133*
Murano, 81
music, 67, 109–110, 110–111, *110*, 133
Mussolini, Benito, 53, *53*, 54, 55, 96

N

Naples, 27, *27*, 46, 50, 51, *84*, 87
Napoléon, emperor of France, 50
national anthem, 67
national flag, 68, *68*
national holidays, 52, 124, *124*
nationalism, 50, 53
National Park of Abruzzo, Lazio, and Molise, *19*
national parks, *19*, 22, 29, 30, 33–35, *34*, *35*
natural gas, 82
Negramaro (musical group), 111
neorealism, 111
newspapers, 74
Norman people, 46
Northern League, 64
Novaro, Michele, 67
Novellara, 87

O

oil industry, 82
olive trees, 32–33, *33*, 72
Olympic Games, 114–115, *115*
opera, 109–110, *110*
Operation Clean Hands, 57
oratorios, 109

P

Paestum, *40*
Palatine Hill, 41

Palermo, 21, *51*, 87
Pantheon, 94, *94*
Papal States, 45, 50
Parliament, 61, 63–64, *63*, 68
partisans, 54, *54*
pasta, 121
Pavarotti, Luciano, 109–110, *110*
Pavia, 18, *44*
people
    birth rates, 88–89
    Carthaginians, 41–42
    children, *11*, 88–89, 97, *97*, *125*
    citizenship, 87
    clothing, 12, 126, *126*, 127, *127*
    education, 9–10, 59, 78, 118–119
    elderly, *13*, 89
    emigration, 88, *88*
    ethnic groups, 85–87, *86*
    Etruscans, 38, 40, 41
    families, 10, 88–89, *89*, 118
    Frankish tribes, 44
    Greek culture, 40, *40*
    hand gestures, 91, *91*
    housing, 39, 87, 89, 117
    hunter-gatherers, 39
    immigrants, 87, 89
    jobs, 36, 58, 71, 76, 78, 87, 89
    languages, 12–13, 16, 47–48, 90–91, *90*
    Latin culture, 41
    life expectancy, 89
    literacy rate, 118
    Lombard tribe, 44, *44*
    Normans, 46
    population, 21, 22, 27, 41, 62, 85, 88
    Roman Empire, 41, 42–43
    Samnite culture, 40, 41
    Umbri culture, 39
    vacations, 117, 125, *125*
    walking, *116*, 117
    women, 55, 61, 76, *76*, 77

Peter (saint), 94, 95, 96
Piedmont region, 45, 51, 72, 122
Pisa, 18, *18*
Pius XI (pope), 96
pizza, 120–121, *121*
plant life
    Aleppo pine trees, 32
    Bosnian pine trees, 35, *35*
    coastline, 32
    cork oak trees, 32
    evergreen trees, 32
    olive trees, 32–33, *33*, 72
    sea grape trees, 32
    variety of, 29, 32
    wildflowers, *28*
political parties, 53, 55, 61, 64
Pollino National Park, 35, *35*
pollution, 36, 37, 83
Polo, Marco, 47, *47*, 133
Pompeii, 24, 106
popes, 44, 45, 48, 79, 95, *95*, 96
population, 21, 22, 27, 41, 62, 85, 88
Po River, 17, 18, 64
Po Valley, 18, 26, 31, 64, 71
Prada, Miuccia, 77, 133
presidents, 62, 63, 64, 65, 68, 69
prime ministers, 52, 53, 55, 58, 59, *63*,
    64–65, 96
Protestantism, 98
Puglia region, 21, *21*
Punic Wars, 41–42

Q

Quasimodo, Salvatore, 104
Quirinal Hill, 62
Quirinal Palace, 64

R

recipe (caprese), 123, *123*
Red Brigades, 57, *57*
Red Sea, 52
Reformation, 98

regions
    Abruzzo, 24
    Aosta Valley, 68, 69
    autonomous regions, 69
    Calabria, 51, 91
    Emilia-Romagna, 19, 45
    Friuli-Venezia Giulia, 69
    governments, 68–69
    Latium, 41
    Lazio, *19*, 45
    Lombardy, 44, *44*, 45, 68, 72, *101*
    map of, 69
    Marche, 19, 45
    Mezzogiorno, 21
    Piedmont, 45, 51, 72, 122
    Puglia, 21, *21*
    Sardinia, 69
    Sicily, 69
    Trentino–Alto Adige, 69, 78
    Tuscany, 18, 47, 50, 75, *77*, 80, *81*,
        82, 90, 122, *125*
    Umbria, 39, 45, *92*
religion
    ancient Greece, 93
    Assemblies of God, 98
    Byzantine Catholic Church, 44
    Cathedral of Modena, 97
    Cathedral of Naples, 27
    Church of Santa Chiara, 27
    Colosseum and, 79
    Communion, 97, *97*
    Edict of Milan, 94
    government and, 101
    Greek Orthodox Church, 98, *98*
    holidays, *92*, 127, *127*
    Islam, 99, *99*
    Judaism, 100–101, *100*
    Latin language and, 47
    Milan Cathedral, 27, *27*
    mosques, 99, *99*
    oratorios, 109
    Pantheon, 94, *94*

Papal States, 45, 50
Peter (saint), 94, 95, 96
popes, 44, 45, 48, 79, 95, *95*, 96
processions, *92*
Protestantism, 98
Reformation, 98
Roman Catholic Church, 15, 19, 44,
    45, 47, 49, 94–95, *94*, *95*, 96, *96*,
    97, *97*, 98, 99, 100, 101, *101*
Roman Empire, 41, *41*, 43, 93, 94
San Giovanni Battista Cathedral, 27
Shroud of Turin, 27
Sikh, *87*
Sistine Chapel, 106–107, *106*
St. Peter's Basilica, 96, *96*
synagogues, *100*, 101
taxes and, 101
Umbri culture, 39
Vatican City, 15, 17, 94, 96, *96*,
    106–107, *106*
Remus (mythical figure), 41, *41*
Renaissance, 47–49, 106
renewable energy, *82*, 83
Republic Day, *124*
resistance movement, 54, *54*
rice, 72
roadways, 8, 11, 37, 74, *74*
Roman Catholic Church, 15, 19, 44,
    45, 47, 49, 94–95, *94*, *95*, 96, *96*,
    97, *97*, 98, 99, 100, 101, *101*
Romance languages, 90–91
Roman Empire, 12, 41, 42–43, *42*, 79,
    82, 90–91, 94
Roman Forum, 62, *62*
Romani people, 86
Rome. *See also* cities.
    art, 62
    Capitoline Hill, 62
    Colosseum, 8, 79, *79*, 83
    language and, 16
    location of, 20
    map of, *62*

mosques, 99
Olympic Games in, 114
Palatine Hill, 41
Papal States, 45, 50
population, 27, 41, 62
Quirinal Hill, 62
Quirinal Palace, 64
Roman Forum, 62, *62*
Tiber River and, 20
tourism, 49, 62
transportation in, 62
Trevi Fountain, 62
Vatican City, 15, 17, 94, 96, *96*,
   106–107, *106*
Romulus Augustulus, emperor of
   Rome, 43
Romulus (mythical figure), 41, *41*
Rossellini, Roberto, 111, 133
Rossi, Vasco, 111

S
Samnite culture, 40, 41
San Marco 1 satellite, 77
San Marino, 15, 19, *19*
San Remo, 111
Sardinia, 21, 22, *22*, 33, 45, 50, 51,
   64, 69, 112
satellites, 77
sculpture, *38, 48,* 106, 107
Senate, 64
service industries, 78, *78,* 80
Shroud of Turin, 27
Sicily, 17, 21, 23, *23,* 25, 26, 35, 46,
   50, 51, 54, *55,* 58, 68, 69, 99, 100
Siena, 114, *114*
Sikh religion, 87
Sistine Chapel, 106–107, *106*
soccer, 9, 11, *11,* 126, *126*
solar energy, *82,* 83
Somaliland, 52
songbirds, 32, *32*
spaghetti westerns, 112

sports, 9, 11, *11,* 32, 113, 114–115,
   114, 115, 126, *126*
steelmaking industry, 75–76, *75*
stock exchange, 73
St. Peter's Basilica, 96, *96*
Supreme Court of Cassation, 66
Swiss Guard, 96, *96*
synagogues, *100,* 101

T
Taranto, 36
taxes, 58, 69, 89, 101
tectonic plates, 23
textile industry, 76–77, *77*
Tiber River, 20, *20,* 41
Tomba, Alberto, 115
tourism, 19, 34, 36, 49, 62, 78, 79, *79,*
   80, *80*
towns. *See also* cities; villages.
   Cinque Terre National Park,
      34–35, *34*
   Cortina d'Ampezzo, 114
   Erice, *26*
   Gubbio, *92*
   Novellara, 87
   Pavia, 18, *44*
   Pisa, 18, *18*
   San Remo, 111
   Siena, 114, *114*
trade, 18, 40, 58
transportation, 8, 9, 11, 36, *36,* 37, *37,*
   52, 56, 62, 73, 74–75, 117
Tremiti Islands, 22
Trentino–Alto Adige region, 69, 78
Trevi Fountain, 62
Treviso, 77
Turin, 27, 73, 74, 87, 114
Tuscan Archipelago, 22
Tuscan Archipelago National Park, 22
Tuscan language, 47–48
Tuscany region, 18, 47, 50, 75, *77,* 80,
   81, 82, 90, 122, *125*

Tyrrhenian Sea, 22

U
Umbria region, 39, 45, *92*
Umbri culture, 39
Unification Day, 52
United States, 52, 54, 74, 76, 77, 88,
   110, 122

V
vacations, 117, 125, *125*
Val Grande National Park, 34
Valle Gesso, 83
Vatican City, 15, 17, 94, 96, *96,*
   106–107, *106*
Venice, 18, 36, *36,* 45, 46, 81, 98, 126,
   127, *127*
Verdi, Giuseppe, 109, 133
Verona, *102*
Vespa motor scooters, 9, 75
Victor Emmanuel II, king of Italy, 51–52
Victor Emmanuel III, king of Italy, 54
villages. *See also* cities; towns.
   Cinque Terre National Park,
      34–35, *34*
   Italian Riviera, 18
   San Gimignano, 80
vineyards, 20, *20,* 31, 122
Vivaldi, Antonio, 109
volcanoes, 17, 21, 23–24, *23,* 35

W
water pollution, 37
Western Roman Empire, 43
wildlife. *See* animal life; marine life;
   plant life.
wind energy, 83
winemaking, 122
women, 55, 61, 76, *76,* 77
World Cup soccer tournament, 114
World War I, 52
World War II, 53–55, *54, 55,* 65

Meet the Author

A LOVER OF CATS, THE INTERNET, CHILDREN, Europe, travel, books, sunshine, and much, much more, Jean F. Blashfield most of all delights in sharing what she enjoys with other people. One way she does this is by writing books on her favorite subjects.

Italy—its people, its art, its history, its land—became a favorite subject when she first visited on a choir tour of Europe during college. The voices ringing off ancient stones told her she would be back. She has since returned to Italy many times and her enchantment with the country continues to grow.

Jean Blashfield has written more than 160 books, most of them for young people. Many of them have been for Scholastic's Enchantment of the World and America the Beautiful series. She has also created an encyclopedia of aviation and space, written popular books on murderers and houseplants, and had a lot of fun creating a book on the things women have done, called *Hellraisers, Heroines, and Holy Women.* She also founded the Dungeons & Dragons fantasy book department, which is now part of Wizards of the Coast. Sometimes, she says, her biggest problem when writing a book is deciding what to leave out because she becomes so fasci-

nated by every bit of information. In fact, she's written several
books of trivia, in which she's collected lots of details that she
wasn't able to put into other books!

Born in Madison, Wisconsin, Jean Blashfield grew up in the
Chicago area. She graduated from the University of Michigan
and worked for publishers in Chicago, New York, and
London, and for NASA in Washington, D.C. She returned
to Wisconsin when she married Wallace Black (a publisher,
writer, and pilot) and began to raise a family. She now has two
grown children, one a professor of medieval history and one
who manages a department at Stanford University, and three
grandchildren.

Photo Credits